From Prime to Prime: A Marginalist Manifesto

Dedicated to Kathryn for reasons beyond even my words

Table of Contents

INTRODOCUMENTATION

My first introduction to poetry as such was in, I think, fourth grade. We were supposed to memorize a poem and recite it in class. I work hard to be lazy, so I checked a few anthologies and chose the shortest one I could find, by Anonymous:

> Algy met a bear
> The bear ate Algy
> The bear was bulgy
> The bulge was Algy

Didn't get any brownie points for that, but I've never forgotten. And, for a decade or so, that was pretty much it for poetry. Nerd-in-training, I was far more interested in science fiction and fantasy.

I was science bound, after all. Kid biologist, I raised tropical fish, taking after my dad in that respect (we had 20+ tanks in the basement), poking around in the woods behind our house, dodging poison ivy and hunting salamanders. By 13, I was making my own agar plates in the kitchen and culturing bacteria in an incubator I built in our basement. I hung around the Columbia University Medical Center and Rockefeller Institute scrounging bacteriophage samples (viruses that go after bacteria). I had a plan to isolate their DNA and microinject into algae cells to see what happens if you bypass the problem of getting the virus through a cell's wall.

Age 15. Sputnik! The U.S. government panicked that the Russian were beating us in science. Heard about an NSF Summer Microbiology Program. Applied and was accepted. No cost, so my parents went for it. Took a train from New York all the way to Traverse City, in northern Michigan. National Music Camp – hundreds of musical prodigies, two symphony orchestras, blue wide-wale corduroy slacks and light blue shirts. "Daddy" Maddy ran the place, Van Cliburn showed up a lot. All these kids bragging they had perfect pitch, whatever that was.

Our program was housed in the biology classrooms used by the on-site Academy during the school year. Ten nerdy guys, all urban, mainly Jewish. Ten no-less-nerdy girls, all from places like Possum Holler, and not. It was eye-opening.

The head of the program was an Associate Professor at the University of Michigan. Number Two, let's call him Bob, was a full-time researcher from the NIH in Bethesda.

Two fateful events.

The Ann Arbor Microbiology Department was one of those places where the only way you could move up to full professor was if an incumbent died. One did and the Department Chair was coming to visit, so roles were assigned. We were tasked to make like happy little worshipful proto-students to impress the Boss. Lick the glassware sparkling clean, as it were. Bummer... realization that scientists don't sit around in an ivory tower all day and think great thoughts like a Heinlein character or Sheldon Cooper. Science was a bureaucratic enterprise – yechh!

And then Bob's research assistant flew in from the NIH labs in Maryland. "You know that genetic experiment you've been running on those thermophilic, sulfur-fixing anaerobes you're 5 years into? Well the thermostats went crazy and they're all dead." Nooooooo.... That is NOT something a 15-year-old should ever hear! I mean five years – most of your fully-sentient life!

So I started taking art lessons that were open to us, went to all the plays put on by the small group of summer drama majors, fell madly in love with the gorgeous blonde who starred in Little Mary Sunshine but, of course, dared not approach her. Not until the very last day before we all left, only to discover that the liked me as much as I liked her... damn. Never got farther than one kiss.

Started reading and writing poetry. Found a classified ad at the back of *Fantasy and Science Fiction* for a little mag called *Showcase*. Submitted a couple angsty poems. Jim Gove, the Editor, liked them and even published some.

Couldn't stand high school or living at home, so I snuck into Antioch College as an early admission student, skipping my senior year of high school, with an interest in poetry and theater. Published more. Hated the campus Poet, Judson Jerome's courses. He was into prosody, and I was not. Later he and his pals dissed Allen Ginsberg when that idol of mine came to campus and lectured on concrete poetry. After my first college quarter on-campus in Yellow Springs, during which I hung around with the drama crew, took a co-op job on stage crew at Buffalo's Studio Arena Theater. Got to work with Jason Robards and Colleen Dewhurst, George C. Scott, Robert Goulet. I was 17. All the old (probably in their late 20s) guys on staff were chasing me around while I chased around the usherettes... nobody caught anybody, but I realized that the theater life was not for me... Too much tension, too low pay, just too fraught.

That was '65. Crewcut men in cars threatened me with scissors because of my medium-long hair ("normal" cut I believe it was called), a friend in a bar, high on dextromethorphan (couldn't score any grass in Buffalo at the time) asked me if I was a "hippy," first time I ever heard the term. I finally get laid (there's a poem about it here). And I met the girl who became my first love (she makes a cameo, as well). Can't complain!

Next quarter, back at Mother Antioch, far too full of myself (I can see in retrospect). Kept on writing and took up my unofficial major in Experiential Chemistry.

My next co-op job, fall of '66, was in San Francisco. Brought a bunch of high-quality LSD with me(coals to Newcastle), took over an attic space from last quarter's Antioch co-op students, next door to the Family Dog house in the Western Addition. Let a bunch of people I met on Haight Street live in my flat, went to the Avalon and the Fillmore, read poetry at the Artist Liberation Front's

Free Fair in the Panhandle (prototype for Summer of Love be-ins the following year) between, maybe, Quicksilver and the Dead.

Evenings and weekends hung around the Haight, worked for these super-straight ex-Army Intelligence brothers in their luggage factory-cum-showroom. Missed the parade when the Feds made acid illegal, bought a ticket but also missed the last Acid Trips Festival 'cause they moved it from the Fillmore due to a plan to schmear the seatbacks with psychedelic-laced DMSO for the Young Republicans Rally scheduled the very next day and only my buddy, Little Joe was able to find it. Between delivering luggage, making up and sending out catalogs, helping in the factory, took any opportunity I could to type out poems on their office Underwood... and I was on my way.

Where? All kind of odd places. Got married, drove back West across the country in my mother's very basic underpowered, cardboard-paneled, radio-free Corvair, busted heading East on the Bay Bridge telling the cops my wife is here but she doesn't have her body on (she was still in the City, wondering where I was), busted again outside the release party for Country Joe & the Fish's first lp (hey kids, don't mix speed and mescaline!). Eventually realized it wasn't a "train to freedom," it was the city jail. Parents came out from Long Island and bailed me out (très embarrassing). Thrown out of San Francisco "by sunrise or else."

Became a Super on NYC's Lower East Side. Studied Mandarin and Tibetan Buddhist texts at New School (really cool WPA murals in the classrooms when you got bored). Walked out of college during the Columbia riots when none of my SDS friends agreed with my suggestion when taking over the Administration building, to bring mops and buckets and clean vs. trash it.

Yoga with Swami Satchidananda up on West End Avenue, (gulp, I'll admit it) did a turn in Scientology hoping to run into William S. Burroughs (never did). Even for a while being groomed for L. Ron Hubbard's personal staff on his Flagship, the Apollo, in Corfu. Flag Chaplain until I pissed off an ex-Vegas-working-girl who was sleeping with Ron's #2 at the time – boy, do I have stories. Left the ship, moved to LA, ended up a top auditor at ASHO, the American St. Hill Organization, got into conflict with hard liners and had daughter #1, quit Scientology and countered with Christianity (did that ever get to my parents, oy).

Moved up Highway 101 to the mill-worker town of McKinleyville in Humboldt Country (well north of the Green Triangle), went back to college (go Lumberjacks! drop them trou!), fell in love with the redwoods and the Pacific Northwest, dodged footlong banana slugs in Arcata. Then down to U.C. Davis outside Sacramento, got myself piled higher and deeper, ended up becoming a *social scientist* (as if biology wasn't déclassé enough). For many years, that killed my poetry (I became prosaic?) but, then again, I specialized in the social construction of reality (or realities, America's big problem today), new religious movements, and growing sinsemilla from the Grateful Dead's seed in my backyard. Started a hypnosis practice only to discover you don't make money telling people you're teaching them how to use their own imagination to take care of themselves. I tried and I tried and I couldn't get a job. At a university or anywhere else. At least I could get high…

Back East, tail between my legs, attempted to work with my dad and brother in the family wire-equipment business, taught Sociology at Alfred University in far-Western NY. Upset the powers-that-be by teaching "non-standard sociology" (focusing on how social science can be used in service of positive social change), teaching courses on the sociology of rock and roll, publishing my own Intro textbook since those large, soul-free compendiums sucked, not dressing like Jimmy Carter in a pullover and tie when I had to tramp to class through three feet of snow, nor following my right-wing department chair around on his jogs with a *Wall Street Journal* under my arm. At least I got to see Seamus Heaney read, but mostly hung out with the local counter-culture artist crowd. They had flavor.

Ended up around Philadelphia for a couple decades doing marketing research, flew over a million miles for focus groups while doing my best to pass as a businessperson (I felt like I was in drag wearing those suits). My marriage somehow survived until it didn't. My ex, wonderful as she was in many ways, wanted me to be Normal, hang out with the "right people," and become a pillar of the community. Well, I never really got along with e.e. cumming's "mostpeople," nor they with me.

Bored shitless, except when I was reading, listening to music (took in a lot of blues, folk and rock 'n roll, had a Philadelphia Orchestra subscription for 20 years), watching Monty Python, Dr. Who, Red Dwarf, Babylon 5, or underwater, SCUBA diving, goofing on the eco-show, took up ballroom dancing, never got very good but it was more fun than working out and psychically more reinforcing...

Major tipping point was I got to meet and befriend some of my lifelong musical heroes, the Holy Modal Rounders and their musical family. In 2003, at a Rounders-related gathering, I met Kathryn Frederick (artist, indie record label impresario, literally a rock-and-roll widow) on her very first trip to New York and... the rest is ourstory. Best thing that ever happened to me – as the poem you'll see in here has it, realization of my dreams.

Got her back home to Ory-gone (as they say back East), got to live among creative people (mainly working musicians) and still do my straight job on the side.
In these pages are my un-edited, un-airbrushed, uncensored, unexpurgated truths and delusions. Psychic (some maybe even psychotic) emissions of my life from then to now. Lovers and wives, dreams and frustrations, embarrassments, and embellishments. My sense of humor, my sense of awe. Confessions of a Marginalist. You might like some, you might hate others. Some are sweet, some are corny, some heroic, some erotic, some are probably crap. Be prepared.

I planned to publish these poems to commemorate my 71st birthday but procrastination and writing another book got to me, so now I'm finishing this collection of poems in roughly temporal order starting from age 17 while practicing "social distancing" as the COVID-19 pandemic stomps across the world and makes me wonder whether Gaia is done, just done with these uppity apes. At least the Orange One lost the Presidential election. Maybe, just maybe, there's enough of us truthseekers and builders, singers and dreamers and creators, battlers against entropy and champions of love, to convince Her otherwise.

(This second printing has been modestly re-edited to correct typos, fix a few glaring goofs, add in some poems I find I'd missed plus two new poems, including, fittingly, a final poem for my mother)

Labor Day 2021
West Linn, Oregon

OVERTURE

MAKING OF A MARGINALIST

I never had Groucho Marx's problem

no group ever invited me to join

that I could spurn

The only first-generation kid around (our

family didn't belong to the country club -

we didn't fit in)

From earliest memory

Mother's endless monologue

recollected miseries, Nazi-

Haunted childhood and the War,

losing her parents, stranded in time

and fascist Italy

Then to Manchester, perennial waif

rescued by my father but still lost

(they'd met in Brussels in line for lunch at the

USO just before the end of the European War

she was in the British army, a translator,

he was a Yankee (!) non-com (!) who heard her accent

Said "I think we have something in common,"

Long story short, they fell in love)

She'd just wanted to get a degree

And study evolution, instead

became a housewife; she did her best

but it was never enough

Enter her proxy (via C-section)

she was terrified to hold me, I was

so small, but precious

The only thing in the world that was all hers

even as an infant I devoured knowledge,

literally, ate those stupid Golden Books,

Kept asking "what is this?"

"what is this?" I'm told

and dreamed

(Of what, precisely, I don't recall...

except being loved for me, myself and

who I was

Not my mother's surrogate intellectual genius child

or just another Straus.

my dad 's very German thing...

He saw the world in concentric circles

more and more Other as you moved on out

from immediate

Family, extended family, German Jews, Jews in General,

Americans of the white

persuasion, Europeans, everyone else

In my heart I rebelled, not

Me and mine but drawn by instinct

to heal the world, that kind of Jew,

Earn your right to breathe the common air.

I hung on the fringes never quite

committing,

Never becoming part of a whole nor

joined a crowd

observing, hanging back, from earliest childhood

Trying my best to figure it all out

by myself,

my parents loved me deeply but were no help

Dreamy and slow, unathletic

From age four on

my meditation, my release and my relief was

Wandering the woods

Behind our new family house in Lake Success,

Along and across the Old Motor Parkway

Once a raceway, now broke down

out the door, up the grade, make a right, keep going

an ancient overpass without a road,

Flaking "To Ronkoma" sign in white paint

everywhere first and second growth

maple, walnut, ash,

An abandoned vineyard, hoops of shaded mystery

under which to scramble when still very small

down the road, to the left

Meadows, a swampy little stream, skunk

cabbage, untamed woods, no angst, no

Weltschmerz, and no trails

it was magic, it kept me me...

there was an old lady in a dark brown house,

'53 or '54, tumbledown,

With speckled hens... One day

an old farmer came up to me and Opa Louie

as we walked the stubbled once-potato field

Nearby,

straight out of a black & white cartoon,

shotgun in hand, overalls, long gray beard and all:

"Git off my land!"

Further along an ancient ash

tree in its secret clearing in the woods,

Solitary, majestic,

"Chas. Lamb, 1854" engraved on its trunk

grown out, barely legible, 15, 20 feet up

From the leaf-scattered ground,

Beyond which grew sassafras and sycamore,

inscribed maple, middle-aged oak,

J.P. loves M.B. 1942, 1946, 1951, whatever,

remnants of campfires with occasional

panties left behind

Later that led to a lot of yearning but

I mainly dodged poison ivy (my nemesis)

and hunted red-backed salamanders

Under fallen logs (avoid the punky ones,

they've got yellowjacket nests)

sold them to a pet shop, Jungleland

As I recall, for 19 cents or was it 39?

once there were two scary, scruffy

older boys who'd arrow shot and dragged

Two huge snapping turtles from my

private, weedy, mostly

stagnant parent-forbidden pond

Alongside Northern State Parkway

just beyond the rusty sagging chain-link

fence with three strands of barbed wire on top

You had to sneak under, and I did

from four till tween,

fearless, fat and full of dreams

THE SIXTIES

FRAGMENTS

(Remnants of earliest manuscripts sent to
Jim Gove, my first champion, in Spring of
'65)

We are chips in the bingo game

but I'll not act like a button

(I'll walk in make-believe armor

and live in a castle of cards

and trust in my dice

      though they're weighted to lose)

and I'll remember Lori's death yet pretend

that there's something to win;

                pretend

I've the power to choose.

I feel the loneliness, don't you?

      I feel it much more:

The hag sleeps together with me

my wife is the wind in a house of dreams

all our children are tears

& the husk of the locust

before he sings briefly then dies.

The air smells like spring to me, though

and we the dreamers come

and saddened we return home;

we go back to our books.

some guest has arrived here before us,

it is the wind.

What remains?

     What remains

  all the bubbles burst

butterfly bubbles the puppy wind tosses

and pops?

Once I fell into a den of Christians

in the Village and

at City Line I saw a doll

hollow, shattered, torn like a corpse

crushed by a bulldozer treat.

Who am I? If you'd like, create a biography. In what

passes for reality I am entering Antioch college as a

Freshman this fall; that is, I suddenly awoke and

became sentient

And all a-trembling, weak and molding,

Ariadne slid naked to the grass.

A LOOSE SONNET

Dark, haunted, is the night, with trees
gently embracing in the drunken sky;
young; setting whispers in the breeze
and all the somber mountains sigh.

Why can't this mountain dance? Because
he's never learned, too lone a one.
but Mt. Stolid holds surprises:
volcanos lurk inside his stone.

A warm late summer's night & some
of Aphrodite's modern daughters
is all I'll need to get me drunk;
I'm sick of standing here sober)
come, flesh, let's leave this mountain world;
let's go where twining limbs unfurl.

FOR JBS

"Cast about in the palm of your hand;
among the pebbles find the sun"

Actress, little actress,
what is this play?
Which scene is this?
I'm confused:
who's prompting me?

"Cast about in the sand of the beach;
the Pole Star lies beneath your feet"

Actress, little actress,
Who's the director?
What comes next?
I'm confused:
who's prompting me?

"Cast about in the night's black flood –
no, you fool, for the dream called love"

Actress, little actress,

what's my part?

Who wrote this play?

Oh, hell, I'm confused:

what's prompting me?

IMMANENCE

The Second Coming? It was no great show,

but a somewhat fantastical bazaar

in some far-off place, like Hitler's Dachau,

where lean Death peddles drinks from his bar,

ancient dreams are sold by the sign of the star

and the Butcher's old mother hawks love.

SCHMUCK ON A SUBWAY

I

There sits a golden hair
covering a golden head – and, I'm sure,
that shift covers much gold besides the visible
(above those sandals, the thick-girthèd legs).
She smiles; I hide beneath my book,
but she's not smiling at me.
her blue eyes behind glasses are glassy,
and she talks to her girlfriend about boyfriends,
and, besides, she's not very pretty
and her mouth reeks of Bwooklyn.

II

And who is the smug one
that's me in the corner,
sitting in the corner
reading a book?
Who steals a look
with half-burning strange eyes,
melancholy weary eyes
seeking in vain what vainly he flees:
old whore-city herself,
(who'd come if he whistled).

DOWNTOWN

Mistletoe dangles from an orange

wrecker's crane and

there are no lovers to embrace

in the gaunt steel shadows

of a city yule.

No snow falls on San Francisco/

Santa hangs popeyed from his jolly belt

in the shower, Virginia,

Mistletoe dangles from an orange

wrecker's crane and

there are no lovers to embrace

in the gaunt steel shadows

of city yule.

F 123

Wine thick air

good cabernet, the good

green smell of spring.

yearnings. Daffodil colors.

Nerves stretching out dendrons

shaking their branches in the first

warm wind.

Puppies.

Puppies.

Frogs and boys and girls and girls and boys

quiet ones and loud ones

laughing ones shouting ones naked singing ones

whispering

running ones merrily jumping ones excitedly

touching ones hurriedly

humping ones and

puppies...

I can't take it any more I'm going to scream.

HOW NOT TO HUMP A TASMANIAN DEVIL

Earth's a nice place for roaches but
you've spoiled it for me
let the Blattodians take over the world;
they deserve it because only they
know what's happening before it happens
and don't really care, just scuttle and run.
we are at the Bronx Zoo watching the Hasidic
families watching the Goy.
Little Karen comes up running and bellows
"MOMMY! the nasty old camel he spat at me
Bawwwwwwwwwwr!"
Mrs. Nebbisch glares indignantly at him and says
"Camel, you ugly old humpy old nasty smelling camel,
why did you spit at my sweet daring goil" (who
is meanwhile trying to pull off the whoosit's bristly tail).
The Camel considers the matter sardonically
a moment then, curing his vast,
pendulous, slobbery lower lip,
he answers with a great mucous gob of spittle
right plop! to the tip of Mother's furious nose.
Which is good Zen
and goes to show you something about camels.

SONG 25 JULY 1965

O death be a pill bug,

life's a puddle

Let's

not

& say

We died because

cicadas haven't mouthparts.

Lie still

(I'll kiss you in

the mud and on your lisp).

QUARTET JUST BEFORE COLLEGE

one; another for JBS

I feel the loneliness, don't you?

I feel it much more;

the wind sleeps together with me,

my wife in a house of dreams.

all our children are wept tears

& the husk of the locust

before it sings briefly, then dies.

It is too cold for me out here.

I am the calf

who is lost in the forest

all the long winter –

o how cold it is, cold,

& the husk of the locust

before it sings briefly, then dies.

The air smells like spring to me, though.

I can see the unicorn

who treads so soft and pale:

the willow frond seems tipped with green

and, yes, the air does smell of spring

& the husk of the locust

before it sings briefly, then dies.

I'm cold; I'll go inside now, 'bye.

always I wanted

to follow yet waited outside

but now the unicorn, he comes –

I'll ride, instead, to the stars with him

& the husk of the locust

before it sings briefly, then dies.

two: between the sheets

Some guest has arrived here before us;

it is the mist,

come as Virginia Woolf's pale body

spun into wind,

come to the wake

as are we,

the undead, unburied living dead come one and all.

Blake come with his angels,

Yeats toting a gyre;

Dante led by Virgil come,

Shakespeare by a lover.

We come, we poets, to the wake

by the ream and in the quire,

we, whose hearts may no longer break.

Some guest has arrived here before us,

it is the mist,

the broken wandering dead come home,

returned to the swamps where the living reside.

And we the dreamers come,

the arrogant, undead, unburied dreamers,

the eternal ren,

come to the wake.

Our kind is laid out in gilt plastic coffins,

buried, no sound but the buzzing of crabs

on the highways

and the choking mist.

Then it's all over and, saddened, we

return from whence we came;

we go back to our books.

three: images for Ezra Pound

I love... you/ he with a whisper,

twining all her blondeness (so).

Theseus... Theseus/ she blush-panted:

all a-trembling, weak and molding,

Ariadne slid naked to the grass

      What remaineth?

What remaineth, all the bubbles burst?

Such bubbles as a child doth make

with plastic pipe from liquid soap;

butterfly bubbles the puppy wind tosses,

and pops

      Every one.

four: song of New York

Little dark girls vending roses

in the city

gruesome plastic roses, "free"

– I like to think them gypsies

really giving gifts.

And I have seen the prostitutes

in times square.

Once i fell into a den of Christians

in the village; and,

at city line, I saw a doll

hollow, shattered, torn like a corpse –

crushed by a bulldozer tread.

(26 July 1965)

THE MINER OF HAIPHONG

(U.S.A.

You astigmatic

Okie who

sought

To rewrite the world

and keep

your stupid brother

under wraps/

Eternal waif

with

pockets full

of blood)

That's not the wound

of the Cross

you

fratricidal ass,

It's

the mark

of your father

Cain.

IF IT WERE THREE THEY'D PAINT THEIR HOUSE RED WHITE AND BLUE

They lost two sons

In VietNam

So they proudly fly the Flag.

THE MARMOT FALLEN AND SHY

I stopped and he did an

we waited, both of us.

some critter stirred

in the early March sun

and I turned my head to

but didn't see.

Neither did he, hunched

against the ground brown

barelybreathingly alert.

I stood here barefoot and

he stood there bareass

but for the fur

                which

covers his shame to be

a woodchuck in the new age

not a thinking waste

basket. how some

men covet that fur,

shamelessly they

become screwdrivers,

jackhammer, computers,

lathes, generators, worm gears

and cogwheels; they wear clothes

to hide their animal skin.

I ran to greet my cousin

having never met a Woodchuck

before and alive but

he took one look at my

naked feet,

gasped and he fled.

BUFFALO WINTER NIGHT

We pressed aside the stars...

    my breast upon yours,

        my thighs along your thighs

            beat. We mingled sighs.

We hid time away

    for a while... and we lay

        quietly together,

            my face in your hair.

I plucked for you one certain Moon.

    red as sandstone

        you leaned against my dresser

            reading from Tagore...

                (Dim recollections of my first lover;
                she had dark, curly hair)

SEAN OF MOONEGGS

(To my first true love)

12 stars were snowseed

steel flowers

suspended

in evening's teardrop sky

and the moon was rising

when we walked together

early in summer

      of an embryo time.

Your dusty eyes gather

an eternity of

Spring

your hips thrust like orgasming mountains

though your breasts aren't full

as they will be when

we wander together

through lands without boundaries

   and years yet to come.

The stars are trembling mooneggs

agates of sunlight

lodged

on the silver palms of dawn

remembering the hours

we'll share together

in summertime and winter

   your thighs will birth the day

[Coda, 50 years after]

But the sun then

faded

into another day...

I'd been at Antioch; you went to Reed

we exchanged one letter and never again did I ever see

your gorgeous handwriting

so carefully fashioned after

Benedict Arnold's (whom I

must have come to resemble in your eyes)

FOR A GONE LOVE

I love you with my skin

or what it bounds, inside

and out:

with all that is mine and boundless

I love you.

Always I think of you. Why?

how might I be "insincere?" Never

(and I trust you).

Why can't you be here with me right now?

... Let's be thankful for each other

time will come we'll never be apart.

I kiss you with my love on yours I feel

the warm curve of your flaring hips,

your fingers wandering gently along my back

(you beside me inside me all over).

I love you. I worship our sum.

that is much – it is nearly enough. why

am I not content?

SQUEALY LIKE A PIGGIS

The rat man desiring to cut your nose off and feed it to

his nasty caterpillar childs sat you on his stinky knee cutting

off your fingers so they wouldn't scratch, you see

and the saintly bat man chewing at your toes thinks and he

gives you his own favorite candy stick to suck on peering not

unkindly through his eyes so you'll stop crying

suddenly you wake up screaming in the dark but Mother's not

there and Father's not there only you are and you are alone

In the big white room and there are no walls

only the rat man there are no walls and no mother and no

father and there is only the horrid old bat man the cat man the gnat

man who laughs all the time giggly ha ha

ha till you feel all squealy like a piggis inside chewing off

your fingers so they wouldn't scratch and he eats your toes and then

you wake up. Where is your nose?

You wake up screaming help me scared in the white room alone

one night turn on the light Mother Father alone without any walls you

can stop with in the white room the big one and where is your nose?

You wake up in the white room screaming and it is night and you

are frightened but nobody turns on the light o my god there is no light

so you had just better face it baby.

(Good Elf Publications *Freesheet Three*; cataloged in the British Library)

YOUR HANDS SO GENTLE STOOPING

Upon awakening while

I'd otherwise have fallen into running

from fear of running into myself again

till night,

I watched our hands so gentle stooping through the dawn

unfold a rose.

Your hands unfold the petals of the mescaline sun

each unfolding gently folding

another flower

into mind.

Your hands unfolded the moonflower and now

in the morning they step

through the dawn

unfolding colors

gently

gently

gently so

(you unfold the blossom of the sun.

Only you have that power,

keep me from fleeing myself forever

into eternity

because only your hands are so gentle as your heart)

which quietly opening through my flesh

unfolds the stamens and the pistils and the sweet sweet
pollen of our delight:

your heart comes gently opening to unfold

my mornings and my nights.

Your mouth opens softly oh so softly pulsing with the dew.

In the morning your lips open

up colors

and the sun

(gently

gently

gently so,

you unfold the mystery of our love.

WHO WILL EAT OUR JOY?

To some days there is no end called night

Or tingling dawn when

no dinosaur lumbers

Through sunny clouds who eats

the joy of children any more now

that we are no longer

Children and never

adult but

we stroll

along the sky in this new age

Of love and pick

up electric fallen stars to fill

our vase of many nights and

days without

time

But only your eyes your eyes

and my hands your

breasts and two jaguars

making love on a windy rock...

to such days there is no end called night

because night is no longer

End but a

continuation.

sunrise moonfall

an abundance of viewpoints.

to this irreligious day and night let

there intrude no dinosaurs

with teeth.

MADNESS OF THE DESERT

Swirling

his sky-blue cape he grinned

Crimson shadows and

offered his luminous arm to the queen

And she took it

running howling through the desert like

A wounded wind lizard

so he died

By the Joshua tree

who ate sidewinders and ants

In hopes of becoming a tortoise

with the bones of a mouse.

LOOP

Doom blossoms. red

white wings

of hopes like these dis

tress me – mind,

null's full count of

sinful sheepdogs.

blow; blow ye undressed worms

laden with dreadnaught's

fiery cake!

        O love

a lucky lily bullfrog west

come over the sandy sky

to thee.

     I am a red-

backed salamander in the

U and S of A but

tomorrow

Job phoenix will burn

for being, what

is a capital offence, eh?

O death be a pillbug,

life's a puddle/

   let's

   not

   & say

we died because

cicadas haven't mouthparts.

Lie still

(and I'll kiss you in

the mud and on your lisp),

tonight

  mostlike the fat

complacent dolor tree

of the newly witch

NAVELLESS NIPPLELESS

What thrill

of the pearlygray breast taste or

my body vibrating to the

shrill contractions of come

with its fountain

of sparkles

wells up through my spine when

her best friend's uncle

mounts her technicolor wriggling ass

unto blackout...

> O god the moment before we come
>
> together
>
> in the white spirit room
>
> and the splashing of mucous!

Where are the flesh bodies of dawn?

navelless nippleless

a brittle sex arises out of celluloid

and methedrine

aching for

the stink of oblivion

and the snap of parting placentas in reverse;

Brittle people

wander through their plastic pornopolis seeking

spinal thrills in empty cubes weird

cerebral orgasms needles and nightmares.

laugh. In all

their sophisticated depersonalized sex they

have never once crossed between bodies

shimmering and touched.

THE NEON WANDS OF NIGHT

Bewildered by last night

in skull city stood

a crab while

a second crab scuttled past

& another & another, all

tidy

wearing sharkskin.

the face of a crab is cast

in its shell;

Shells rippling with faces

torn & broken.

another crab drags its carapace

into view &

another & another, all

waving blank anemone eyes.

one crab only sees,

with clenched chelae – his

antennae lurch

trembling

through the coughing air.

the stars glow raggedy amber through

purple clouds over

skull city where

the neon wands of night

transform

human ghosts of day into

crabs, crabs

clutching attaché cases, gray

crabs shuffling by in parody of day.

Crabs swarming secret tunnels plotting

the assassination of

moonlight.

This crab stops and spasms (his eyestalks

roll upward and just

in time: black fiddlers pick

moonbones with fungus

limbs).

Crabs scuttle down the streets of the city.

this crab's shell splits open

in the jaundice light of terminal dawn

revealing a long

pale man

& a soft young girl.

More crabs scurry past, gray

shell after shell, all

clutching their cases. one

crab stops, extends

a hungry claw tearing new flesh

& another & another &

painting a mandala of blood, we

joined the sun's corpse.

MORE FUN AND GAMES WITH PLASTIC

Last Thursday Bullshit Andy said to me "I

am a wordfreak – I

scrape the delicious glistening words from my

nickel bag of dictionary pages

and dissolve them

in a spoonful of warm, lugubrious grammar.

sometimes I add an extended metaphor or two

for kicks,

then I shoot the shit under my eyelids

into the forebrain.

He nodded off into abstractions so

leaving his polyethylene cubical at the Post-Graduate

Crash Pad I met

my sweetheart in the park

by the Horatio Alger monument.

she wore white jeans and her hair fell to her waist

softly

a pale brown gentle beyond words.

FROM A LECTURE BY GALWAY KINNELL

He was naked and he stood in the bird's song

of the conifer grove and smiled while he

flexed his twenty miracles in pink.

that broad monkey face wrinkled; he smiled;

he giggled; he laughed; he burst into laughter,

convulsively shrieking, I am!

As he walked alone into the sunlight,

his second lyric poem formed:

sweet is my woman/ to be is to love.

Old Adam stood in the ruins of my house,

bat's wing over bone, naked;

his ravaged lips were cracked like mud

but his eye still bright.

Damn you, people of this house!

he spat, like all the rest, you died

because you lived in fear of love.

Pocketing his heart, he crossed

past hope, past tears, to our neighbor's house.

DEATH OF WINTER BEACH

On a beach (not so very far

Distant) in another world

I watched a flight of golden bats

Break from a maple tree

In the wind.

Something has filled the empty rooms

Of my mansion with its presence

& I stand on a beach

With you beside me

& Walk with you through the wet streets

Of a magical city

After long rain.

Three little boys in yellow slickers

Stood in the cable car eating

Black raspberry ice cream

Cones dripping all over

The floor.

Seagulls wait for their time to come

At the ocean's edge

& They have always waited there

On one leg.

A swimmer dips and bobs in the cold

Muddy bay, look:

His white cap is a tiny whale

Surfacing to smile at us, hello.

On a branch in another world

There are no solitary gulls,

& The worm becomes a moth & leaves

Behind his apple to be a golden bat

In the sun.

It is good.

It is good.

It is good to stand here on a

Beach with your eyes smiling

All over & the sun hanging in the sky

Where it belongs &

There are seagulls standing on the shoreline

Waiting for their time to come.

The trembling sea calms

As clouds disperse after heavy rain

In the San Francisco afternoon.

The death of my long winter has come (I hope

And pray) –

It is good to sand here on a foam-decked beach

With your eyes smiling (not that far,

After all, from tortured metal crying out

From skyscrapers

& The whimpering, car-trammeled roads)

Good to feel you here beside me

In wonder.

NICE DAY (THURSDAY)

Spring has sprung

leaping for

my throat

clawing

cloying

stinking snarling

breath seeking

my heart,

pelting me with

plum blossoms.

FOR KAREN WHO CRIES

Elfin

beauty out of sight in

toadstool moments of your eyes

Dreamy and

your voice among angels. I

have never quite seen an angel but

The giant night alone

with stars

seen frosty days and frigidly

Clear waters

of the Western Ocean sniffing

at my feet (hell

Nearly freezing them off

my first visit

to Stinson Beach)

Alone?

You are alone?

We are all alone here together and

The sky the sand the sea,

purple sailors heaped

in their myriad solo voyages' cul-

Mination and all the starry horses

grazing in the meadow of the night above.

Alone?

Let (o listen to me I know I know)

bitter griefs' past pain in

the river of your tears dry up

reach out, come close

and, if only for a brief and stony, soon-lost while,

dance with the angels.

FOR NANCY ALONE AND NOT THE RABBITS, GEORGE

Green green green is the ever unfolding

of our nightly moment returning the gold

in the sand the time is the never yet oc

hre joker, joker stained crimson begetting

pain pain pain out of the green is the

never never refolding refolding of this worl

dly torment resounding maize voice of

the sun sun sun sun

'BUBBLE BURST, THAT'S IT"

This is a lost never never never to be for

given secret inside under the pillow of

moonlight loudly loudly screaming OUT OUT

OUT through the roiling shadows awakening

heliotrobus and still knowing for the flo

wing flowing flowers indigo maroon velvet

weeps weeps weeps angry joy shouting oh

green green green is the always folding of

folding of flowers!

(Please,

I would love to know you

softly in

this world so

please come back if

you can

forgive me)

and she did and it was the end of Winter

STUCK IN A REAGAN FOR GOVERNOR PARADE

Ron, the Candidate, smiled

& his wholesome strippers threw apple pie.

he will give us plastic faces!

cry the Bankers,

wagging their dollarbill tongues.

he will give us plastic faces,

said some clerk to me

& had a heart attack on the spot

& got trampled into the sidewalk

by a dozen red white & blue-nosed matrons

chasing William Blake down

New Montgomery St.

with frowns.

O it was November Fools

when the bandwagon played Mammy

& Samuel S. Backwards danced

Soft-shoe just like he did in the movies

& with the tickertape fell Adam.

SONG OF THE ANCIENT MANATEE

bellowing at the stars

in a splashing of plankton

foam with a

shiver

of

drowned galleons moon

rippling wake two

humpyback

         'd whales

leap out of the sea gray'

belly to belly writing the constellations

they copulate

        high in midair

because that's how humpyback'd

whales do it and they

drop back into the

sea, exhausted

and panting like the salted sky.

SEARCHLIGHTS

O my time and spatial love

    Let's

        Weave

    Such

            Electric patterns in the sky

    Of

        Nylon

         Woes!

THERE ARE MANY THINGS TO SEE

There are many things to see

In the sky &

    Touch

This lemon sun

With your fingers dear.

Was it a sun?

It quietly changes like a pale

Dream of the sun

& The image is moonbeams thought

By a gentle child who

(There are many things to see

  In the sky)

    You touch

My chin

With your fingers, we embrace.

SUTRA FOR PRINCESS WHOM WE DIDN'T BELIEVE

I am the Lord of the wholly whole

who has gone, gone

gone beyond

desperation

and returned here

for love. Bodhi, svaha!

I am the Slave of the Holy Whole

who changes who touches

who switches the dreams

of lovers sleeping

softly in the past

Princess seeking through 16 years

wandering

so much nothing and hollow

and dead that you can't go on

without light

without light

or at least

without love.

Princess tossing and stung by the bee

buzzing restless meat bleeding

out desperate love

love

into night

wherever you are

into night....

I sigh.

Princess reaching out to that other realm

realm of weepful times no-

place where miseries keen nothings

under raindrops

comes a light

comes a light

laughing

comes love.

Princess lusting hard like turtles

soft like your breasts

trembling

and young as this breeze

singing night

singing night.

it's not right

I sigh.

Princess writhing half insane look

with your eyes: When everything

goes, something

returns, moonlight and

sunlight

and someone

and sunlight

And love.

I am the Lord of the wholly hole

who guards the bridge past

time and emptiness

nightmare lies

sharp craggy dragons and

the puddling fear.

I am the slave of the Holy Whole

who slew the nights

of nothingness

the knaves of loneliness, the weeping of

the queen of tears.

AND THE WIND BEFORE THE STORM IS FIRE

Lips of fire in the wind laughing
against the wind dancing
with the wind

Making love in the face of the moon in fire
with the wind

For the wind is my opposite sex and my mate
in the form of a jaguar and
I am a jaguar

And I am the cog of thunder and the wind before the
storm is fire
and she comes to me with flared nostrils breathing fire

Reaching with her mouth of fire
and I press back mightily against the wind
belly of thunder

and the sky dances through us waves
of fire

Striking off my eyes
and the earth is a fury of trees and even the clouds
are writhing

Feet of frenzy and claws of fire
my form is thunder and the wind

Before the storm is my mate
and this is our moment
I stand

Face into the wind a universe of storm to
press into the wind wholly

And to dance the
dance of
flameless fire electric

Jaguars mating in the sky and
our child is storm and my mouth is

Thunder and our child is the beating of the sky
and the wind is the woman
of the sky

And I am the father of storm and
I am the jaguar of fire and

My mate is wind
and she comes to me with flared nostrils breathing fire
thrusting with breasts of fire

Making her pregnant and
we dance
two jaguars

Writing on the face of the moon in fire,
the masters of the universe of storm.

ALEGY

Perhaps the histamines of reality

have percolated through

my evers

so long that always

Perches on my brow

squawking

words of truth and wisdom and

Shitting wherefores

on my why:

So many poems have gone unwritten, are

my dreamways clogged?

BLUE BALLS OF THE SPIRIT

Oh DAMMIT
my muse is out, ran
off to San Francisco or's
visiting with relatives
in Greece.

The bitch is taking her summer
vacation and,
by the balls of Hairy Krishna,
poetry is blocked without
her!

Stardancer, come home
I need you here within me
now.
I'm down with the spiritual dropsy,
all artichoked

Up inside with foul-smelling algae,

bepimpled,

broken,

overrun by dactyl-footed diatoms... by

the earwax of the Buddha,

I need help, I need help.

Imago-homunculi like bee swarms

in my paraprostate (sex gland of the imagination)

and I can't make it without you,

firelady.

Mind comes fragmentary visions,

disconnected swirls

that short of ecstasy.

just can't get my spirit up

without you...

it's bad for my self-image in fact

it's pathetic:

Here I stand a limp and lonely poet

spirit painfully engorged,

not to mention distended.

ASSUMPTION

Dreamking

mounts

the pumping

throne

His red

clown

screams

screams

screams:

Dreamking

mounts

the pumping

throne

his red

clown

screams.

ALONG THE OPTIC CHIASMA

Actuality slices into my eyes

cuttingly

shearing like an unenchanted sword possessed

by a gray and antique

accountant

whose

pale unhealthy limbs are like

a stewing chicken's

and

it hurts – terribly,

like death I imagine

like dying

i need my dreams, I live on dreams

food is a mere formality

I live only

by dreams.... my mind churns them out compulsively

continuously

blue

or clear sparkling silver

passionate soft dark dreams

visions of eternity

and

the cold hard wind

of reality

skewers the heart of my dreams

MEGAMOUSE CYCLES

Scraping small twitchy feet in my closet

where I keep the stars

Megamouse

devours the moon.

A porpoise peeking into my cupboard

watches fear panic the mouse to circles

crash into some gray bags of inchworms

writhing on the shelf.

So pop back through his loophole

to escape that carnivorous glare.

Morning drives up in her wren.

I scrupulously reassemble

our polystyrene universe and sea

the moon is lost with all mystery. A tiger

Paces the sky

And I spin my wormy way

trailing myself forever through his fierceness.

Purple fish of sunset break the horizon.

drop a tab the tiger's gone

enter

(Rampant & Terrible) one Mouse.

(FUTURE. PAST)

Two by two we rose

From the mud

My

Mother, dear mother, mommy, o mud

O genes

O beautiful helical me-making

Molecules

O DNA, mudborn in the sea, o god

Fish, we were fish and weepers on

The sand, eyes in our mouths

O mouths and bellies

Eyeballs in our mouths!

Swamp frogs rolling in the muddy bay

Screwing evolution into reptile beasts o

Teeth, o teeth

Holy teethfulness of my father

And shrewlike we skulked and apelike

We made love and bellies in

Our mouths o mother

My mud

Bulging in the belly, manlike we rose from the blood

& the mud of our mother

O god

What genes

Cranial cavities, lovely cranial

Capacities, lots of room

For $5 words

With fire and rolling on wheels we came to challenge the unknown

(Roar of trumpets, visions of the Roman

Army and huge flaming sunsets.

It's only a movie.

The audience puts on their coats and exits, blinking)

NOTES ON AN AIRPLANE

High
(my god, the
Chronic dog whistling, the
Incessant bull elephant roar)

Hung up on the inside of
The sky like a moth,
Swallowed by a million dollar
Whale cigar.

Scar tissue
Landscape passes away
Below us.
Who burned the earth?

KISS OFF?

When I looked into your eyes I saw
only the image of my face.
I realize now

That I was madly in love
with my reflection in your eyes

You were the stream and I
Narcissus
making love to myself endlessly

A slavish union, rotten jellyfish
on Golden Gate beach.

I look again into the memory of your eyes
and see my own face.
You thought what you thought

I wanted you to think –
please understand this faretheewell:

I look into your eyes and see

the image of my face

Is sad.

BROWN RICE

My bird like a

         big soul

  and

my soul like a

         snowflake

    thrusting

wings out dances toward

         the other

  shore

  .

         (published in *Star-West*, sometime
         around 1969)

SHAGGY DOG SUTRA

Sitting in lotus by a stream

on a hill, Yellowrobe

is dreaming

That he does not dream and

the hill erodes into a valley

eaten by rains

His shaven head still

shines with ghee

dreaming on

The never-ending dream unbroken his

downcast eyes shyly seeing

into other skies a

Gentle smile blossoming one hundred years

beneath his nose while the valley

he has graced for kalpas full of eons

Breaks

and bends up

into a mountain and

Lichens spread across his robe

yet he sits there his dream

unbroken and the

Mountain

grown old now dies

and he is all that remains of the mountain

Draped with yellow lichen a golden

Buddha carved out of immortal

flesh he sits there

The girlish eyes downcast and

palest hands folded

in his lap

That smile

still growing

underneath his all-compassionate

Nose while the sun

grows dim

and the Earth begins to drown

In ice, dark matter,

and a blizzard of air;

Then our Buddha's smile blossoms

And his eyes return and

he opens his

mouth

And out flies a butterfly laughing at the stars.

O

Come silence

nightflower above the sea o come

enfold me come

Silence

o moon who wings

through sleep through dream o

Come slay the dragon-ants of gabble

That drag me from peace

With

Fingers of flesh and lungs of death o come touch me just the once

with your feathered breath

enfold me gentle

In bliss

o let me come go and fly

with you high among the stars

Across this terrible moaning sea o silence

come please smother me

with light!

THE ONLY ANSWER

The only answer

to the problem is

to

metamorphosize

into human

butterflies and go winging

singing

      into eternity.

TO A SLIM GIRL FROM OHIO, WITH LOVE

Among

the fleshy leaves

of this tree

      dangle

its fruit.

There

is nothing you

can do

with an o

sage orange but

smell

      or hold

it in your hand,

dear girl

SHY GENTLE

Come into my eyes shy gentle

fishes flickering colors

of rainbow dreams

Easily

float through the sky languidly

thinking their slow

Rainbow thoughts

flowing

with the silvery wind come in

Come all the way in where

fish can float through

the sky

Slow and gentle just

to kiss you come

into my house through open windows

And down the hall with me

to my bedroom, sleep

my love and dream

With me

shy gentle fishes gather round the sun

and the moon, taking courage

Swims into day

(it is late afternoon we

could dream forever

PARENTHESIS

(You

  must come first if I

 Am to come

at all)

CUMMINGS GONE

Snow calmly i (little you-me)

gentle the stars

(and keeping is doting

and nothing and nonsense

it's) hazel

eyes casually dreaming.

To-

morrow begins at home

(death having lost the universe –

 but that was yesterday).

If a littlest elephantangelchild

should meet

a green jaguar what

might have been? (JustSpring?)

e.e. cummings

the clouds in your post living hands

the sun in your eye seeing.

i wish i had known you.

we might have been friends.

AM PURPLE

There are very few things
exciting as your touch. There's
the sky

Puffing sunlight in
the pipe of a slanty afternoon and

Of course
there are your eyes
which remind me hazel of themselves just

Dilating wonderingly at the old
silly nightmare nested

Plaintively under your bed
and your mouth is likewise
exciting, more so

Because she has talked with the

little people grownups

Always deny but who never

grow angry

just smaller and smaller till all ten

Thousand of their great mystics might

lie dreaming in your ear

O your ear! It

is also exciting and your knees

they are exciting and

Come to think of it there

are very few things as exciting as you

Are taken together

all at once. At

any rate, come here I

Am purple to kiss you and very

much excited by your thighs.

IN THE BESTIARY OF OUR EYES

Greengreen ships of

happiness float through the sky

in your eyes and your mouth

is the happiest home

of a merry platypus tongue who

Grubs for sheer delight

in the meanderings of our love.

your teeth are moonwhite little

coral reefs, along their

Palatal Archipelago flow

Whisperings

of Captain Wonderheart among

the Tonsil Islanders

Who all the time

were making love or eating

Poi. We Americans,

humans, creatures

of the parrotfish joy all

turquoise by day, in-

heritors of nameless men the

Green motherbird earth

the arching moonwitch and of course

the sun whose warm fingers stroke

the down on your neck always

so gently, do

Not eat poi all the time or

chew betel nuts or

any of them savage things. Our

wonderful technology

permits us to

Eschew such unpleasantries as

Betel nuts or

finding taro, pounding poi

so we don't have to sit around

all the time eating poi but

We let the fools outside tinker

with their idiot toys while we

lie here smiling

in the bestiary of our eyes and

all the time make love.

ROSE TOMBSTONE

Another path unwinds through

swampy days of flesh)

when you

close your eyes to the windy

Sun and tell

yourself I am weak, I am mortal(ly

hoping for a

dropperful of

Pity) someplace

in this head.

they canceled out the free radical "R" in their

chemistry equation

It was a conspiracy

the professor was a front

you said,

squatting on the dusty table

Hiding in the storage room

Georgina and her sister wrung their hands

electroshock and methedrine

nothing worked.

An impotent god.

Geoff...

another young face on the wind (wind

wind sadly blowing through Yellow Springs.

SKUNK TZU

What were you doing out in the daytime

and so bedraggled? If you

only had stayed a

while I

would have combed your long black hair

stroked your stripe and

given you a name but you

were very wet and timid and

wise, you saw me

thinking and

ran –

you are a very Taoist skunk.

THE SUICIDE SPECTAULAR OF PETER RUSSELL

Things of shadow

Vague ambiguous traces

and dust

He found nothing real and

deciding to fly

he fell

To

his

death.

Satiated

much now and panting he

picked his body up

Tucking it neatly under

one arm and

left

Peter Russell

and

left

Old dreams

to flap in the moonlight

fading

Things of shadow

vague ambiguous traces and

dust.

He jumped howling

with pain

(loneliness whistling

Down his spine Chicago

wind shivering the flowers from

his soul).

His world

like mine or yours

just things of shadow

Vague ambiguous traces and dust

only

Peter was different he'd

Flow

tight and tensely like

a reptile

Snake never asking never telling

just sitting in that chair

and smiling

From straightjacketed eyes

Inscrutable eyes.

Sometimes

A light in those weird eyes

in that burning head

– suddenly

Her blouse off

and his pants

and

He'd be inside her but

that didn't help

no

You could see it inside him all fungus

blue spiny hard like a

cactus egg

You could feel it crawling

there eating away

his eyes

And sucking his brain.

All his friends found love but

Peter found pain

So he'd disappear,

that

Was Peter –

Knock at her door

and bang away for a while

then just

When she was coming he'd

be gone

for a day a week an hour...

This last time

he disappeared

forever,

Peter and those mammoth feet

those incredible frog

feet sprouting

From an average body

with rigid eyes,

Dayton State in those broken

Spheres

screaming squirming mouths of electroshock.

Peter

Who kept bloating up

tighter

only in death

Letting go:

one leap off that big throbbing penis

passive like sperm

Are to mate and fuse

on the white

white

Hard concrete exploding

and to

die

Satiated and full

at last

he left us

In vicarious and splendid

orgasm

sweating blood white white white the

Creation of

concrete

art

(He was

a poet, too –

she

Collected

them)

white

White

white

death

And the moonlight

where

does one go?

Old dreams

flap in the moonlight

fading

Things of shadow

vague ambiguous traces

And dust.

(Published in *Showcase*, 1968)

WHITE DEER BLIND DEER HELIUM HORSE

And the deer
white deer, blind deer

Helium horse that flies
through the rain came

To blind you in
your sleep

With his starlight from Galaxy
14

And you sought to ride her, breathing
hard running on the tops of

Trees but she
like a helium horse can fly

Through the rain while
you are only dreaming.

TRANSCENDENTAL ELEPHANT

The helium horses whinny and yell
trampling the stardust

Into wind,
the transcendental elephant passes slowly

By the Earth.
Flower screaming

Stay away
the starlight doesn't know

Her language,
touches just one

Petal once
and is consumed.

Little spiders dance
inside a cloud of rain.

The helium horses whinny

and yell

Trampling the stardust

into wind,

The transcendental elephant passes slowly

by the Earth.

GENERALLY SO

It was always the same
        everytime
                I meet you:
You are strong
        you stand unbending
                in timewinds and
Unsoggy
        in the same sleazy
                rain

Always coming down
        (or something
                like that)
You smile
        and sparkles
                leap

Through your eyes into my dreaming
        (fey,
                faerie,

Of another world)
        you dance
                with your body

Or without your body on
        and I fall in
                and my dreams

With your dreams
        raise little dreams
                who dream

Together dreams
        and cuddle
                and then I seep

Inside of you and I find you soft
        and scared,
                alonely as I am....

NEVER AGAIN DREAM

Jewel of the San Francisco dreaming blue

lotus of our acid creation o

Jewel in a lotus but the

wrong lotus a

Lotus of

ice

.

Perfection so subtle and we were un

sophisticated in the matter of jewels and we

Bought the wrong lotus the

lotus of glass

Who

can live in such perfection?

Spring

time for dreaming

And redreaming the end of

all this dreaming now the green bear sleeps

And now he reawakens o yellow is the highway into winter but

our lotus came dead

.

White sexual union of acid and flame

in yellow and blue lie only

One dream and

I say

Bear don't awaken but

never again dream but go into bliss o bliss where can I find you

.

O jewel of perfect changes

light

Where is the end of all dreaming

and the dreaming that we do not dream here

Jewel and the yellow skull in the green bear's flesh all
resolving into light

.

Lotus of bliss lotus
of egress

Like mist round a jewel
and I am the light of that jewel of light

And the eye of the lotus om sheathe me in brilliance I
still am not home

REST OF THE 20TH CENTURY

FORM 150 LOOP

tapping on my window

a little man said Bang

you're dead. said I

o no... not now, be

sides, I

have not the least little

quarrel with you

or your friends.

it's War, said he with a

bucktooth splay grin,

you are dead

admit it

and fill my quota.

I laughed, so I'm dead!

but why not use a gun?

he said that he'd bleed

if he shot me

and shuddered:

violence, why then

he'd have sinned against

whatever is holy

in the sky

and more so

in tomorrow.

I offered him tea

but he stole away

saying visit sometime.

In the mail,

today

I received an

Uncle's invitation to

slaughter myself

in VietNam

I:

THE GOSPEL ACCORDING TO THE NY STATE ASST. COMMISSIONER OF MENTAL HEALTH

'Life as we know it is a competitive affair. If one lacks the innate strength to compete he can... turn to psychotherapy as a means of freeing himself from the handicap of inferiority'   James A. Brussel, MD

Business suited gorillas claw
at their neighbor's throat during the
5:00 rush.

(Published in *Showcase*, 1970)

AN ERECTION OF THE SPIRIT

Thus:

and he comes for you my dear tap tap death

comes tapping a white cane

                and he comes for you with a

hardon baby

              tap

tap tap skull is death's mask for he has no face (it's a film
loop with variations) and

when he comes

            he comes black

            pictures of the carnival he took

himself

my love, last time around

and you die

         As in Shakespeare flopping around the
stage for 80 years or

         so and then you lie still in the hollow of your

skull

and watch the brain die and you cry "i am no more"
and when the audience has gone

you get up

        and you leave that theater.

        But death

has come to you tap tap and death is a conman and his
voice is black silk and

his semen is absence of light and he has conned you my
darling

                                                            but

good.

      Death has come in you my dear

tap tap tap he has shadowed you and he has snatched
you

                    (14 April 1970; rejected by Robert Bly
                    as too academic)

ECHIDNA
Kent State University. May of 1970. Death

Retinal vultures
                of the 100th generation
endo-reticular bullets in their guns as a 'precautionary
measure'

Tending toward Armageddon as the 2nd derivative of
transorbital mongooses first
                            ate the sun up
and then the dawn

Having run out of teargas they shot all 4 dead in one
stanza I
Saw the photographs it was
                            pure science;
let us substitute I the closed interval from life to

Death
as a fudge factor
liberally laced with bloody hashish
                            in the sexual algebra

Ahimsa
but you have broken that promise and as a result we
now find ourselves in Cambodia on the back
                            of a letter to
Nixon.

Blood rushes green and slotted down the old seminary
canal
Poor coeds
            they impregnated you with lead
which we now integrate into your original equation thus
the product

of being born is always death.
                              Don't shoot me mister
the very idea of rebirth gives me a migraine headache
for example

                         is the ejaculation of bricks
the proper Spiny Antibody
of Australia and New Guinea having a tapering snout
and long wormlike tongue in Riemann space?

                              No!
the calculus is adamant
integrate death with death the hypothesized monster is
invariably
anti-life

with an extremely short stubby tongue re: which
we may mediate upon the absolute value
                                        of retinal vultures
and four bodies emptied on the once-green quad-

rangle at Kent State
with a domain of uniformed mongooses crying ibid ibid
ibidem.
Such are the mathematics of
                    the ballet.

C.F.
Chuang Chou (d. 3rd Cent. BC.
                         However see add. Ref. under
Butterfly)

as death approaches x makes an impolite gesture
and cries
                                             Hey
Rube!
What good is a mermaid all she got is tits

Prefrontal geese
                    honking northward in the spring a young
man's anger
turns to rage
and he sees pigs everywhere

but that was before the peacock crowed heralding a
sniper
and they fired into the crowd
                              trisecting the old quadrangle
with blood.

Ballet dancers on both sides of the fulcrum
everything factors
                    into us and them
and there are a lot more of them.

Male platypuses chasing rolling friction down the
muddy bank
                    in the sexual algebra
all aggravated by the war in South East Asia.

For these reasons I oppose sending our troops into
a locus tending toward infinity as a minimal
                    octopus
horny beak the seed varies from place to place drifting
on the wind like fluff.

(Published in *Showcase*, 1970)

HORNY HARRY HURRY HOME

I'm so tired of
everybody's sexual hangups not excluding my own

This one can't come and that one's
scared shitless of getting

Penetrated by some terrible swift sword and
Alfred dreams of pissing

Inside her
and Marybeth fears all men who

Resemble her father e.g.,
have balls

And Janet's waiting for that big brutal
football player in the

Sky to fuck
the shit out of her so she

Can go pregnant and
imitate a cow

But Hermie hides in the bathroom with
the Playmate of the Month

November solo
on the skin flute

He's out to get into her pants and
she keeps notes

And Elsie's lubricant's the wrong consistency
and Jane wants two condoms, foam

And a diaphragm to boot
he proved impotent

While Jack knows that to have sex
is to take something from

Jill who knows it too
and becomes therefore very protective of her

Cunt. You know,
everybody's hiding,

Well,
that sex is smelly dirty awful (intriguing) but

Not really all that much
fun

No, if I want fun I'd go maybe
to a party and get

Bombed, you know
it's like a *duty* something you gotta

Do and then pretend like
it was a big thing

I promised Tim and Joey I'd lay some chicks
out here on the Coast

Ummm-mmm
                foxy

Please pass the clap and Oops
I'm preggie again

26 hrs fucking on speed
and got all upset over it and so did he

And they were absolutely miserable
she'd never screw her *friends*

Said that wd harm
their relationship,

Such as it was
nothing at all here you noticed? About

Love
you got to get laid on the sly

I'd leave her if she got laid by somebody
else how could you do

This to me, Harry,
it's something to be blackmailed for,

something to hid
that Bill was still able to get

A hardon and consummate with Marie having
been wed blissfully these 16

Years to Selma
whom he loves dearly and the kids

I am free therefore I fuck
and the very thought of nudity causes an erection

Marriage is a sort of
permanent installation lest he/she find a better lay

Elsewhere
That's all you get married for, isn't it?

As if sharing were improbable,
as if you could really tell which body

Was which and belongs to whom
as we dance together

And ourselves draw near,
as if it were forbidden to touch you

And me one
another a plural

Singularity
(as it is, isn't it? They ask

HB 1970

And ask that old grouper

in the swell belly

of Ocean

about water:

        "Am young

yet growing older one

day I will grow up

turn belly skyward

Feast for flickering spider crab,

little shark-toothed

gobies"

rambles on 400 years, slow

And doesn't notice when

you left. Go clod, ask the white

moon about sunlight or

the sun his secret opinion

Of space

no answer for 10,000,000 years –

solar flares here and there

several sunspots, a yawn, but

You're gone. Eyes

ingrown and watch the time

flow driven by the Engineer,

go, a golden porpoise

Who smiles very quietly throughout.

trap him in an

ivory cage drug him

and demand what he knows

About life before

death wait forever, that

smile will follow you forever; turn

turn around snarl

And track it back to its source

like a pack of

bluetick hounds baying across eternity

go still

Drives the eons onward. If a blind man

could see I would see your love

dancing like a butterfly or moth

beside me everywhere.

8 MO.

It's impossible
to write a poem about Ericle

She's too full
of flame and wonderfully cool

Ericle-ness
or isity and too damn fast

To catch in a verbal
flow.

Besides, she's so masterfully
laughterfull

I can only
say she's Ericle

Hysterical, my everywhere always very un-babyish
magical happy imp.

ERICA IN DIAPERS

The moment we shut our eyes

she snickers

        wets

or in her special Lingua Erica

cries TIT

Some helpless infant!

3 weeks old

she runs not one but two perfectly healthy grownup

bodies

     yours and mine.

EPIC

Gautama Siddhartha was my friend and

he walked among men

while I held back as always.

Maybe I was the Bo tree

probably I was just afraid

you'd unforget me.

Ghosts

cry from ruined star to star

he has betrayed us!

But the war program remains

visible to recreate and to win for

we have never really forsaken our duty

Only stumbled

over my left feet.

I type, remembering old history

And an epic even I forget.

the beautiful sadness of the ridiculous,

ungrasped, unrealized, unlost.

FOR BASHO (ROBBIE OR THE OTHER ONE)

Dreaming breeds
no beauty

The lotus
casts no shadow

Light is born of
more than dreams

Flowers do not just grow
but are nurtured

Blushing, I thank you
for these blossoms

Who were never yours
(although you dreamed

Them) ever ours
always their own.

THE PARABLE OF THE ANTS (A TRUE STORY)

I took acid once

in Burbank, California and

literally got into some

juicy watermelon. it

was a revelation.

not so much when I met God

while peaking

but when,

coming down,

i stumbled back into the kitchen

toward epiphany:

If you don't clean

Up after yourself,

(this goes for all of hu-

manity) He

will send his ants

to do the job for you –

lots and lots of crawly

swarming, pullulating ants

HEAVEN?

I don't know for whom

God weeps

but were I he

I wouldn't bleed for my human

children (they

deserve the grave they dig,

The eternal comfort

of a warm

bomb crater) I'd only weep

For relief

that the Thief's Night is

now and in the morning

Will my sheep be ingathered (and they

will be much astonished

to see one another)

And there shall be one shepherd

one fold

and no murderers.

HYMN & HYRR

Turtlecloud thunder

eggs

hiss beak sky

Shell you we I planet

mouth sun

wind

Food

star puddle body bomb boom

life game smiling

Spirits

holding "hands" and

playing

A STILLBORN TEAR AND DRIFTWOOD

For Tsura

There is a sadness who is naked;

a little tree smooth now

and pale,

Cold blows the sea wind in a sky frame of gray.

Walking might help,

a long walk...

(Red beneath the crust

We are so thin)

Sand dunes spangled with strawberry plants.

My hand, yours

a stillborn tear and driftwood

Beach, icy water breaking in

from the darkness

Obliterates our footsteps wiping clean the sand.

We are so thin.

there is a sadness who is naked:

just turned one

the child of my friend has drowned.

(3 May 72

Published in the *Annual Anthology of College Poetry*)

FOR WILLIAM MORRIS WHO'D HAVE HATED IT BUT HE'S DEAD

The good little scholar thinks

good little thoughts;

he knows what he's supposed to do

and does what he ought.

But the freak, that bad boy,

he smoked pot, he dropped LSD

and he no longer scans

in ye olde prosody....

No way, man.

like

I'd rather write poems 'bout my old

lady's ass

Than compose sonnets

about clouds

and roses and the tinkling dew

bedecking a shepherd's toe.

Coda:

Lady, it's not that I mind sheep

dip or

heraldic odes –

I mean I really dig William Morris – but

My favorite image's

a dinosaur,

to wit,

your clitoris.

TRUE LOTUS

It gets too same some

times,

    eh?

whatever (or

eternally thing becomes merely

a cloying

un

    unreal

    unresponsive

    unalive)

      and you

get sick of it,

dontcha?

Reality is a fad

    passing

    Reality is today's

      most glamourous fashion

come a new season

we must purchase new eyes

else comrade and scientist

put us down.

Daddy Daddy buy me a new

gestalt, my field equations

are all out of

style and

my good friends all put me down.

He flips, of course. Never!

cries Dad.

If they were good enough for

Feynman

they're good enough for you.

Consequently

Junior loses respect.

Crawled into New York Org seeking substance

Only to get fleeced

by the typewriter in the sky –

not so much the Commodore

but all his self-dealing

henchmen.

One down, time for another path

look around

empty beercans

empty Book of Thing

empty temples of the hour

and day a

hollow heart

shadows flit like lizards

among ancient clay bricks

crumbling under jungle.

Weltschmerz has driven us out

to the edges

seeking a True Lotus.

And who sniggers?

Amphetamine hurriedly rapes

your spine

heroin slowly

rolls a yellow eye your way

ethanol plays patsy

with your liver

while Dr. Acid gives you a vision

of lotuses

self-referential lotuses, fractal

lotuses forged out of ice

that melt into weeping

if you touch them just once.

Legion old men and women, doddering gurus

      each invite you with an obscene

      gesture (technically a mudra)

          Come sample my lotus

price one billion years

              servitude,

costs nothing but your you,

free just worship me as avatar or Lord…

      buy any, try a few

      I did

Even tried God

all chapters in that same old Book of Thing, new cover

reformatted, rephrased, regurgitated

same old Thing.

You get rather sick of it.

Hollow hollow, hollow is the Lord

of (fill in the blank), every last Thing

he is is empty.

      O wanderer

          explorer of planes

brambles and soft flesh

come home!

  Something alive

    something responsive

a true lotus longs to blossom inside you and so patiently

(if only I and you and we could find it)

      (1971, revised 2018)

NEW RIVER NEW DENNY

Ouch

blast it

my foot!

Slippery

stinking

stones,

Water

Colder than

A meditating

Eskimo's ass,

dawn air

much colder.

Snagged my

line,

lost my lure,

Bail screw

just flew

off my reel

And sneered

at me while

scooting

Down the

riffle

causing many

Trout and

maybe a

steelhead to

Shimmer

with laughter,

shattering

The first

sunlight

and my dreams

Of a lunch

without

peanut butter.

(My last little mag poem, 1973)

[　]

How do you do?

I am a nothingness of fire.

ALWAYS I NEVER

I

Always
always and always I never
heard the pinetree into magic
lungfish go
suddenly animal and
panting softly in the night air reach
out hungrily
grab a star.

II

Damn, damn, damn,
the rainy poet thoughts, big
bloat clouds hovering approximately
nine
feet off the ground and
in my head all
dripping saltless tears
and birds.

III

My wings

my precious interstellar butterfly

wings

so new so wet I never

sailed the moonlight

or charted flower constellations

in the just-before-dawn

my wings.

IV

This morning I un-

folded

this morning I unfolded

my fragrant dreamself

I did and I

smelled the timestream,

learned to undream,

in fact, I opened my eyes!

V

Little hopping groundbirds

squeaking and a monstrous sun

is sunning chipmunks

on a rock.

Behind you a

dogwood trembles, very slightly,

dreaming of when she

goes naked with the moon.

VI

I have found the quiet of the earth

Shhhhh! And who is shouting

gnats and alligator lizards, beetles, porpoises

and bees and the mating song of

grasses (blade beats upon blade)

and there is peace here o my gentle gentle

love, now

o now o now o now now now now and forever!

THE GOOD NEWS ACCORDING TO ME 1:1-8

In

the beginning

was the Word

And

(among other

 things)

the Word was

a pun.

THE POLITICS OF REVOLUTION 1

The politics of revolution.
a broken cat
curled on the landing, should we stay
when they put her to sleep?

Cut and dried
it blows away in the wind but
the wind itself
takes a while to blow over.

POLITICS OF REVOLUTION 2

Revolutionary fervor crush the flowers

and shoot the pig

who accidentally crushed

a planet.

POLITICS OF REVOLUTION 3

Black man

white man

purple fur

would handle

the problem

nicely.

PROSODYDUMDAH

The entire

                    purpose

of

            my poetry

is

                        to cure

your constipation!

UNFORTUNATELY TOO LONG FOR A BUMPER STICKER

Strong
            Long Wong
      Sunflower
                  lashes out 3 times but
                        misses
            the sun.
                                    Quick, man, run!
Thick hands writhing
      epics
                  of panics, heroics
            denunciations,
            frustrations.
Yellow face
            burns
                        churns,
                              a glowing
ember,

            turns seeking any enemy
                  who blasts it
      into November.
Ah, sunflower, weary of war!
your sharp
            shapely
                  little teeth
      they gnash
            and they grind
                  as you stand
      in the front lines
                  of dawn
            and then
                        behind the line

of this terrible

                        marching year
            and its sidekick
a nameless creeping fear.
            We abide,
                we abide in stuffy boxes
        wet with the dew
                        and damp
                            with our own
perspirations.
we are all POWs
        Only
                    What war is it this time?
            Who are we fighting?
        Who are we?
What for?

COELENTERATA

A specific jellyfish,

                          it goes without saying,

sees nothing wrong with a jellyfish

But,

        Of course,

a certain Mrs. Adler

                      Seeing

yet another jellyfish that Sunday,

whilst wading

                at Jones Beach,

Screams "Oh my Gawd"

And runs away.

Did you

ever wonder what the jellyfish think about

        that?

CENSURE

Sun heaven shud

der sorely close

eye nak

ed corpse all nak

ed nerve so nak

ed flesh also

no skin bleedy bloody

of time now

time then time when all

gone big moon angry

white star sickle

raise point

glaring most little finger at you.

IN THE DARKNESS OF EVERYBODY'S BRAIN

Do you see me squatting

with my pants down

frozen

in a child's nightmare?

THE BEACH AT MURRAY ROAD'S END, 1976

Planet, time

and Mad River carried mountains down

to the sea in little

pieces and

On those bits grew

wild strawberries and flourished and flaunted

white flowers

a thousand years of perennial snow...

To the North Coast's mist

gave the greenery color

In almost weekly rotation

yellow and blue, purpose and pink, shy lavender,

Red, orange and while, and pale,

pale green. OK.

then old Mr. Buzzard bought a piece of paper, see, and
said

"It's mine, all mine," and went and mined it.

Oblivious to sweet August's tiny berry

and the pungency of miner's lettuce

and the sobbing cry of birds,

down to the sea

With trucks he came

and carried off the dunes to pack

a sewer system's concrete pipes

because every progressive community must shit cleanly

Through sanitary sewer pipes

and the sand was free

and who would hear the screaming of the mist,

the outraged river grumbling in its bed?

Oho – what's this? The cavalry to the rescue, folks,

environmentalists armed

with television news footage

and class action suits! Ta-da,

Buzzard halted in his trucks, the good guys win , they win

at last.

But the river was Mad, madder 'n hell,

it tossed its serpent head

And writhed a coil

and moved its

mouth a quarter mile

and blotto! The beach was gone, bequeathing its berries

To the bullhead and perch.

which goes to show you that the trees who fall

in Bishop Berkeley's forest)

couldn't give a flying fuck if you and I are real or not.

IN VIOLATION

I plead
innocent to charges
of seeing the moon in
the late afternoon:
it's not poetic.

INESCAPABLE CONCLUSION

Each and every (shudder) time I
get myself
                    involved in business
        poetry happens

(all by itself)

Business, these facts suggest,
might be America's but is not my business
                    (dreaming is/
        ghost dancers and butterflies)

QUASI-SONATA FOR ONE HEART'S TREMBLING

_____

Ghostly I touch

you   is it?   And tremble to sing birds

in the tender emptiness of

secret

        You

across print and page

fei ch'ang tao nor with parateresis

when i lack both

face and

Finger   when I am ineligible for the merest

shadow. I

fail to burn my joss sticks

at the shrine of the spirit of the age.

Om

        mani

                padme

phat.

Phat.

       Humbuggery ah/

Hurry harry hurry hurry home

shanti

       shanti

when there is no shanty

only a tarpaper palace or

                     give

us this day

our daily

       Phat!

       Phat!

FATUOUS

       Complacently silly, inane.

Lord Buddha yer smile

is

       well, simplistic.

had you known   (yeah,

there was no-one there to tell ya. Yuk yuk...)

that smug grin

Would be tinged with sadness, sadness

sadness

    and a different

        joy.

_____

    I do not know how to write the way

    awarded poets do

    or ride

    Spenserian geldings

silver and

bronze,

reflecting through nighttime's mist

    splendor down purple ribbons

    of darkness over snow peaks/

    versifications

    in the form

and formalities

Of the Great King's Court.

I'm just an ex-suburban bumpkin from beyond the moon

    who rides a leafgreen ass

    and knows no

    graceful words direct from heaven...

    just a pale spooky human

stuttering tales

of flitting

quick wonders I've met

    in the lovemaking of our smiles,

    the tinkling sound

    of sunlight.

How can my thick white male words spat

clumsily into the wide spaces

of your eyes

leap unhindered, little panthers

    coursing through the meticulous

    diaphragms

    across your control room

    door

grab you and shake you

Hunched with your lights off in

secret masturbations

    on a lotus throne

    you've never seen – please,

    please, look,

    please:

So wondrously carven of ivory and diamond

precious jade and the jewel of space time

shimmering as graceful

holy and pure

    (as you are

     as you are

     as lightning reflected in midnight snow.

_____

Beloved

beloved

you walk in your garden

unseen;

your ten-thousand lovers each

loudly boasts

his conquest of

your virgin heart –

But their eyes

are dim

therefore they lie. Neither have they touched

your shimmering face

or

having glimpsed the veils of your gown high

up on your candied mountain

once

by the merest chance,

they took another sip of moonlight

that turned away their eyes to the valley

of a lowland mistress

and named her by your name.

I am so few and they so many and they giggle

saying

widdle widdle whatisname

he would cuddle with phantoms.

And lao ren

Lao

Burns three joss sticks at the shrine

of ancestors/

His sons

sneer at a stupid custom and shoot

their pearls

out

into the warm, forever empty cleft of darkness.

POET

Mouth eyes paint

the dancing twinklepoints

of mystery

Passing for dust motes they

float across the sky

invisible as a herd of rampaging elephants

LAMBENT LAMENT

Everybody else's got connections
where I don't even have a plug
everybody else's got black magic
all I have is useless love

Everybody else's got the knowhow
where I don't have a clue
everybody seem to know the way,
all I know is how to dream

Everybody else knows all the right lines
I don't know which way to turn
Everybody else's hip to Secrets
I give up, I'll never learn

Everybody else's got connections
where I don't even have a plug
Everybody else's gorged with worries
Foolish me, I've just got love

Everybody else's got the knowhow

I've got nothing but a guess

Everybody else's read the Guidebook

all I've got are my own words

FORAMEN&FORWOMEN

Foreknow&

Forego

Foresee&

Foreswear

Foredoomed&

Forwhat

Forgod&

Forcountry

Forefather&

Forefinger

Forauldlangsyne&

Foryourbirthday

Foremost&

Forensic

Forkicks&

Forethought

Foreleg&

Forearm

Foramen&

Forwomen

Fourteen&

Forthehellofit

Foryou&

Forme

Forsooth&

Forever

Forshit& (yes, baby)

Forshit.

WHIM

Supposing I had some

leftover time

should

I use it to patch up the world or

maybe take a few years

and live on a mountain

in China

7,000 years ago?

RIPPLE RIGHT ON JILL

Wave creeping cross wave creeping fade

Jill

snakedance weave body grin over space place slow

bubble sneaker kick lock centipede

blind mind boss across

lotus now

in band-bang spacetime waltz around

the feary hen

who lays galactic eggs.

In chaindrain pain rain roiling bane nerve-scuttle bound

Cosmo-John and the Man

with the Black Machine

bend

bent tone agony drawn bloody noodle soup snap spill
flash

flesh crackle eternity wrench green centipede fangs drip
drool

dribble claw break and balloon burst 1-2-3

Jack the screaming star fell

into sequence o rubbling bubble stomp electric squirt
and squirm

Sperm gell into Jill of the kick hair

and scarlet yes infinitely of

a vaguely inhuman form and antiform across the
multiverse

dance madness serpent coil belly hair grinning

snake fingers

crawl among many stars seeking the other

Jill oh

John oh circle flickering pictures in a hardcore position
dare

we take it dare we do or don't

In through flaming claw

bubble hammer throw dream scream

squirt on naked spaceless face fat and timeslime

hand stretching

through

a closing portal fails to grab the little red rooster –

snake dance weave time grin over space will this next

egg prove infertile squirm we're off

and on through wave cap wave writing ripple right on Jill

Kick to hydrogen screech

amp billion trillion scraping space end bunny-hop bang

beat green centipede feet kick claw John

whirling dizzy dribble sneakers scratch scratch scratch
the naked fabric

across heavenly shell rip crack squirt grovel oh dig I do

I fingers crawl snaketime rock that spacewarp roll I do it
do it

do it do Dr. Albert Einstein

plays a Stradivarius accompanied by Rabindranath
Tagore on veena

in the corner aquarium.

THE POET 'SNOT

Now

popping out the junkie's arm;

Hero

or heroin who forms

Into pretty pat

terns un

Usual permutations of nothingness on

paper so as to pre

Capitate p-

sychic organisms or at least

Turgidity a

nothing being with laughter. No, a

Poet 'snot some ordinary

mugwump but

Differs he got

tickly feet in brainpan

What dances

out mind balloons 24hoursaday

Unceasingly to shimmer

under in

Terior sunlight

and he

Got to

grab holdof them flutterly bubbleflies very

Gently by der probo

scis cage them wordwise

Whom

in his eyes, ears, mouth, nose,

Gosh! And caught which

perfectly out like a stone brujo aiming to

Hit some other terminal case o'

Re in

Carnations' rose

or sunflower and peni

Straight zing

o

Smack dab into yon
der soul

making said in
dividual to explode furiously in

Fit of apple
plexy

peach pox, star dandruff or
preferably

"Goddamit what
the carrot-chewin hell

Am I still doing
here?

Pardon me,
I proceed to split."

And splat –

he gone man,

Gone beyond. Ah so,
my kinda Poet 'snot

Just anybeast but special
what

Transmits, communicates,
Infects

You with glorious sadness, frustra
Tion and the malady of incurable laughter!

SAPIR WHORF EXEGESIS

Why do you hide and

why do you cry or

why do you hold caring so close

to despair?

Why is your world all

bloody and raw, a big toothy

wolf-eelish maw,

when all I am trying to do is to share

(With you the hidden laughter of bright winds

beyond the utter edge of alive

and the smiling of moonlight dancing

downwards wildly through the naked sky)?

Why do you sigh and pull down the cold

damp dew and hide

amongst cobwebs when time is so huge and

there's no where to hide in,

Life being so wide that

we're all inside and for those who would dare

to nakedly care (to love) there's

no word "blue" versus "green" nor verb for "to die."

SHE WAS A NOTED ENTYMOLOGIST

Open up each child

of winter learn

to undress.

IT'S DECEMBER'S END SO LET'S CLEAR THE OLD IMAGES
LIKE DUSTY

SPIDERS IN YOUR GRANDMOTHER'S TRUNK

I wish

it would all come alive, the walls

remember and the stars

shake off the darkness built

of leftover

turkey.

ZEN JIVE

And smiling we walk out into infinity wondering

where our heads would be at if

we had any...

HORNED SUN

Moon slips in naked between surface and sky
silver finger

        tweaks

           the green nipples,

fondles sensitive hilltops.
she stirs,
        leaves rustle in halfsleep, moan

           betrays rising pulse of mountain

ocean,
stream, lawn

        and valley, every vine and tendril

          surges outward.

earthmouths gape.
moon writhes

        pointedly against gravitic aura

        till Earth awakens.

Breathing

hard, she grasps firmly

the Moon's ray

and strikes it deep

        into her kingdom,

            and again

and again smiling;

And the Moon beats against earth into orgasm

                spurting dreamstuff

        white, white

white,

splashing against bare rock, gardens,

        dim trees,

           white beating down upon the

ocean.

LOCUST ELEVATOR STORE OF A TRILLION YEARS' AGGREGATED MASSES

A trillion years aggregated masses
trembling
on the locust elevator into
                        Allegory/
        Cicadas exploding regularly in rush hour swarm
        out of darkness
                        down the one-way street
        grabbing for the sun they coat all the tree
branches
        forming entropy apples
                        to fall on your head.
                        Satori!
Swat...
trembling
                little couples begin their grateful song
and still trembling they die.
        Does this not strike you as
        bullshit?
When you go out into the June to squish
cicadas under your sad
feet
        please make there be a silent miracle
to happen
amid the sound
        of crunching footfalls
        Ananda,
        and shut your mind down
                        turn the volume knob
        to the right
                until you hear a click.

PITTBLE JON

Squirmf deside yr jins & rud owt lood hoh boi th

lible (goodsh) betwnn r legs it say

redificial flavr took sover th worl

yis yis yis hooroy!

Si boi, I god it all in mine book down;

the imiltation momma race yu on thet mechicotti

soo the chilgrow intoa man desiooring nothing mor

he he as a good lay. Pur Jonny Americoo,

ya truck around hoping it exist,

pitiable Jon, ya wants nodding mor as a good lay/

      Can ya dig thet?

        Wow!

Fooxy, baby!

                        So yu arsk r,

      Bable, art thou a good lay?

Uh? She slamb ta halt on r honeypunch whils

stair in thruy yr shades ril cool wiggle sey

      Yis, I am Big Boi,

        and we got spechal plastic flavrd tits to

pruv it.

Gusj!

Ya aint nevr met an Article befor (ho dear).

****

ME FOLLOW ACRICOONS, I INTERSEC DIS

POME FR SPESHAL NOUNCEMENT.

DIZ BERY DAY, DIS BERY

SOME DAY,

ORGYNG IN FLUMMY SUBURPAN BADROOMS

DOSE SENSITIV SLURBS SNICKR CRYPTICAL

BOOT LOOR & UDDER!

SMELLNGK, TAYSTNGK & (I WILL B BLUND)

FEELINGK!

CITIJAMS AMERICOO WER BILD OF.... &C.

AN I, POLYMR P. PLASTIG.... &C....

IF RE-ENAKTED WILL &C....

AND &C...

THANX BERY ALL FR LOANDING DY EARZ

YU MUCHLY, &C. GOOB NITE.

****

Pooey.

Yr tox dingle in thr tennie shoon. Muchever will

th nabors thimk? Wll id

drov poor Dayd t drnk or is e ded alreddy?

Growping thru yr shadled eye to hr will ya evr

rilly no fr shur &, Jonny, do u wanta?

Oooo

yr scalb prinkles & yr bowels growel,

yu b wonderfully wht flavr...

      Gee, dat's swit, Jonny, but why wonder?

      Diskover!

            Cum wid me awoy t m

psychedroolic

          dom & (shih

tayks yr handl moyst)

Yu screem,

      Gangle m jorb! Shih goes awl I won

danyhoo!

    Am like r n th scrortch,

        Banzai!

    ****

    GLOB-FEELINK AMERICOONS.... COHESED

WE

CONFORMZ, DISCRUPT WE SLIYD INTA GOO!

EET M BOI

OB DAT GOOD SPALSTIC MUSCH.... ONCT

CLISS, STINGKY PIGINS FLISPEKLED TH

WHOOLSM AYR, WATR'D OOZ FRM BG

SORZ I TH GROUN (UGH)...

LETTUC TANK TH LORF DIS DAY FR

POLYESTOR...   OIGGLESNIT!

PLASTK PIG PROPAGANANDA! LIBERTATE

DE OBBRESSED TAYSTBUDZ VON DIE

TROWNDODDED MASSHES...

SEYN DE STINKLESS HOOM 2 DA CRAKING

TOWR! STENCHBOMPS N THAIR DUCKS!!!!

QWACKIN GOVRFOOT & UNDRHEAID N TH

SITTY CLOMP CLOMP CLOMP ARISIN FRM

DA

SOOERS A MILLYON WEBB FOOTS

A MIRCHINGK SUNG

BLU SKYE

AZ WOND A FOICE OB D PIPPLE CROWZ

RADIFICIAL FLAVR TOOK SOVR TH
WORL!!!!!!!!!!!!!!

****

Dum brod, he eth whool carze?

Evribobble nos whn y tern em ovr deyr awl

a saym anyhah – oigglesnit!

soo ya got chrerself 1, Jonny ol biin,

an yu gottr aloon (heer goes)

so yu drg er off droolink 2 yr umpty
bangabed

bangk bankg

but shis not the lay ya bin lucking fer,

Damb thet Radificial Flavr,

Crap!

Orwell, anoodle day anoddle lay…

yu

fone the amulanch & dribble off

inta d smoggy borning certain

grimble grimble

as somebod isomewhr haz mayde a mistak.

GREAT NECK – AND MUGGY

Inchworms drip

from

fatty maples the grey

heavens broil

        jets

sweat blood across

them

      broasted chicken

with rotor blades

beat off

against the sky

and chart the overheatedness

     of cars during

rush hour

filled with grey

       androids

blank as the sky is

perspiring home:

That's life?

LITTLE BLACK SPECKS AND GREASE MERINGUE

Newark sky cytoplasm

streams industrial

thick congealed soot wafting

unlife manufacturies

it is something that affixes

to the hemoglobin

and it never leaves you

noon

behind the factory

diner

(grilled hamburgers ketchup and egg salad plates

thick coffee)

in the parking

lot

where

mighty dragons

paw the asphalt impatient for fire

in their bellies

the day they elected a black man mayor

something had to

change

cadaver grease

and flies

from the underworld

golem chassis spilling out

of the junkyard

through the caved-in fence

decorated with flies

grasping

At the Cadillacs and other

shiny monsters

`   with

rusty wheels

something had to change, man

if flies were algae it was a very

stagnant pond an

aerial sewer scummed over with

little black specks and grease meringue

inside, the diminishing employed bitch about

bosses

tossing soggy french fries at their

overwrought tonsils

something had to give

the spirit

of pink slips grinned in the soup

the spirit of man lay down a tip

but the spirit of magic

entered tiny morning glories

threading the parking

lot who incredibly raise their

clean snowy heads up

against the flow of grim soot and

laugh.

TIJUANA IN NY

(For WSB whom I never met)

Tijuana in NY (Los

Angeles) (Yellow Springs, O

hio)

Old Doc* staggers

up to Hank,

           fibrous hand lands on

Jonny's shoulder. It has drifted

there. "Hey –"

and we never saw Alice again.

Eyes

wise about the central darkness

staring out:

        "Psst......"

dragonfly or fingers dart

down and back to Doc's

own flabby breast-mounds (observe)

with them he draws apart these halves

of flesh slowly

exposes a heart

-     not his own, of course; and the pacing
      was excellent throughout.

"Meester,

          I show you the Secret of the Universe?"

Thick

not unlike

shag rug

the landlord hoped wd raise the rental...

*He'll

  sell you the same thing

  forever.

"Sahib! Come,

this fella he lead you to the One True God."

Hank (Peter) (Alice)(Harry),

would it matter** if I'd stop

time dead

right here for you and now and write

in bold caps on the sky

THE OLD DOCTOR'S GONNA GIVE YOU

NOTHING (absolutely

nothing) FOR FREE

** When he fingers your lapel and stops

   you in the alley (on a corner

2 FLORAL POEMS

α.

How the

     Hell do you

  describe

morning glory sex?

β.

Instructions:

     grasp firmly your

     fragrant dreamself and

     unfold it

SUTRA OF ONTOLOGICAL PHENOMENOLOGY

Reason

    (however elegant

     toothsome,

     divine)

won't stick

to your ribs,

he said

(munching a dream

 with soft

 tantric noises)

POOF THE MAGIC PIFFLE ON THE OTHER SIDE

Atten—hup!

OK,

hand in your wings.

        HE UNSTRAPS HIS WINDS AND PLACES

    THEM BEFORE HIM ON THE GROUND.

        HE STRIPS OFF HIS FEET AND

PULLS OUT HIS EYES

    SETTING THEM

    ALSO

        NEATLY ON THE WELL-

MANICURED LAWN.

          HE BURPS UP HIS HEART AND

    SNEEZES THE BRAIN OUT THROUGH HIS

LEFT NOSTRIL.

    UNPLUGGING HIS PENIS HE LAZILY

    REMOVES HIS BALLS.

        GENTLY HE LAYS HIS SPINE UPON THE

PLOT BESIDES THE LIVER

PEELING OFF TWO RATHER COMMONPLACE HANDS.

Drumrolls crescendo.

The Guardian struts forward deadly
    serious
    and is about to pluck
the belly-button
when

    POOF!
    HE WRIGGLES OUT OF HIS SPIRIT
      UAL BODY AND
        THAT'S THE END OF MY DREAM.

TRÈS UNCOOL

In trying to keep all my eyes open
and proceed gently

    I don't know why

    exactly, it makes no sense,

    but I always do

I tend

you see to trip over my feet while

stuffing them into my mouth –

which is definitely

not cool.

I long to tell you that I

prefer breathing in

your proximity

that this friendship tickles the belly of

reality making everything smile

and my enjoyment in our

friendship goes

so deep it's high.

whenever I should tell you these

things, I choke up.

I wish I knew some deliciously archaic

fully ridiculous

and beautiful tongue in which I

    might confess how

    natheless

my body suggests

other ideas about friendship and proximity but

that would be inaccurate, Lady

I like loving you as I do.

So what if you make me horny and this poem is
pompous, bloated and absurd,

I feel good just being around you and glad that we are
friends.

forsooth, my backyard's not the only green in Eden,

you're proof

that there's someone else or more to enjoy

joy with whom

in the fullness and vagaries of time.

Which is more than ok.

I am loathe to endanger what I fear (perhaps foolishly) is

the fragility of our relationship but there's a closer and
more friendly that, well,

might be nice.

O damn. In trying to keep all my eyes open

and live gently

I tend unfortunately

to ping pong back and forth outrageously

between playing the fool and

being an ass

if only I couldn't or wouldn't or didn't –

I know, but I do

and that's not only a shameful tragedy of maybes,

it's très uncool.

THE CAMEL'S SPIT

        Never hump

a Tasmanian devil

          although

the exercise might do no harm

            look

before you leap

        observe

what you are getting into

it might bite.

MY SPERM RUNNETH OVER

This spermy met an egg some day
said hello

                I'm yours
        you're mine

                    Oops
            o God!!!

        You're me
                I'm you

And they grew
into a tax exemption.

10.4.72

Amber

    Amber

      Amber

             enter crying

with blood and joy and wonder mingled as

your mother smiled

your father kissed her

    and the doctor stood amazed.

        No

     this child did not leap up

into an oratorical posture

and exclaim

      "Today the Scripture is Fulfilled,

          Let the Triple Worlds rejoice!"

     I don't recall an

            earthquake, flight

  of eagles

or eclipse....

Rather, Amber suckled at her mother's breast

     and the doctor and all his

   nurses

said it was hypnosis

as they put away their syringes and

   equally silly things (unused).

we laughed at them.

        Of course

  it wasn't hypnosis

(we kissed again)

  it was love.

SUN QUEEN

The glow elephant jeweler crafts sturdy

dreams of white gold and

filigree

Like dancing snakes

a tiara on the brow of

          the Sun Queen.

The hippos whistling tend their garden

of wishes and asparagus

                  grunting goddess

     Of the leopard-spotted sun

your glory takes form in the dawn display

wind turtles

And dolphins tinted transparently pink

or gently blue

        dancing in celebration of

Your many faces

        as they change you

change

The process is called "growing up"

the sequoia blacksmith forges toys of molten

      star-stuff

In your honor

so we laugh happily as we change your diaper knowing

      you're no baby, no

              Your corona

flares all gloom thoughts into daylight joy

the wonderful alligator who

Comes in the evening with bunches and bunches

of freshly cut wishes

            baskets of dream he

Bows and

calls you Goddess of the Sun

      the sky is in your eyes

          And your eyes are in the sky

you are the Sun Queen

the baby is a mythological beast

ENTITLED UNTITLED

There, across the bay of milk white water

(actually his glass of

Ouzo)

snow calmly

he sits gentling the stars. You stare,

What the hell?

WE WERE TOO TIRED SO THIS POEM LACKS PRURIENT INTEREST

A big white starsized elephant eye

was not seen last midnight

in the western sky

and no small galaxy died in

my sleep

with a sound of tiny trumpets.

I held you but lost,

my eyes raced me to close, winning,

your hair tickled my

nose until

it wandered off someplace lined

with black velvet along with my mind

THE UNSOLVED CASE OF A DOUBLE MURDER NOTES UPON

Who put the spanner in Mrs. Murphy's gestalt?

Jim doesn't care

he's dead

I suspect

they practice murder as a goof

and die by profession and

that's only human.

Little flesh.

Jim doesn't care

he's dead.

poor bastard, he once tried holding up a bodega

with an ivory soap gun

totally out of character, must have been stoned

on smack or speed but

somehow he got off that time, not this,

no getting off this.

No getting out of this.

He's dead.

Impotent spirits gnash flappingly

      above warm meat dead.

Sweetums twiddle while a poisoned dog

dies dead.

One of these bastards later killed Jim Sharp

And the girl, squish their faces.

      Never hitchhike with a human

it ain't safe.

      Go find myself a mountain and sit on it forever.

Hell,

I think it's a television show

      starring Everybody Else.

THE RUSTY TYPEWRITER SQUEAKS

Am a poet still or
do I change from this self to that else by
not doing?

Is a poet what he does or what she is or
how we smile upon awakening
or merely on who opens

To admit
the sunlight's bright
moonlight's silvery sharp caress

And stench of whales beached
in time and space
upon coasts of stainless steel

Self-regulating beaches grossing out even
the seagull who
cannot find a place to drop a clam

Assuming he had some clams which

he does not nor

can he eat beercans.

Is a poet the way she stands or

how he sits on the pot or

the way we move when not otherwise occupied

Then with the forms and permutations

of life?

Is this a poem or just a pile of shit

Or are all poems shit or

all shits poems

written by creative intestines to some

Jade alligator wallowing coldheartedly

in the bowels of New York City

watching time's sewage flow

By, waiting for the Second Coming of

Diplodocus,

liberation from mammalian oppression?

REPORT ON THE EFFECTS OF PORNOGRAPHY

All these years she's wanted to see
A dirty movie so we went
To see one.

In Paris once I almost conned her into believing
The Graduate (in French) was a hardcore
Flick but she caught on.

Diane finally got to see a porno flick.
(The cosmic conductor raises his baton, his
Universal orchestra builds to crescendo

In good Viennese style)
She'd left her wallet at home with her ID
The old woman at the door almost didn't let us in.

"You want to see my stretch marks from nursing two
babies, lady? I'm 27."
"All right, I trust you," after a long blank stare.
"Just I hope you don't get into trouble"

(Rolled European "rrrr.")
Snare drum goes tap, tap, taptaptaptaptap,
Baton comes down, hard.

Marilyn Chambers has ugly toes

There was the big black stud, there was the fat lady carrying a tiny pig.

Lots and lots of bodies pounding this way and that.

Semen squirting everywhere.

No smiles, no laughter. It was all

Very serious.

The lumpies behind us were really getting off.

Uh. Uh. Uh. Uh. Uh. Uh. Argh. Uh.

Uh. Uh. Uh. Uh. Ooo. Uh. Uh.

Uh uhuhUhUhUHUHUH

Ugh.

What a drag. El bummer –

We couldn't touch one another for a whole day without gagging.

At least they didn't have any foot freaks

In the movie, so we could play footsie.

AT RINGSIDE WITH HUNDI

Knowing people

knowing dogs

why didn't Christ die

for the golden retrievers?

FANGED IMAGE

Daylight

comes bouncing in

Like

a wooden bear.

UNTITLED EVERYTHING

How

bu hen hao

who cares hao I will find you?

Fei

ch'ang tao nor with παρατήρησις; I have

already quit the human race

why is it then

the memory of you lingers?

Touch me again (right here)

And I'll

     Figure this out.

SMALL COMFORT FOR BILL AND BRENDA

Almost

tentatively

indeed, now then gone.

Down

      down

      miserable heart

      there is no

      place

for you in my poem.

Come time, come reason wash away

the little breathing

(barely)

      lovely unlucky

      (or lucky

       or was it luck)

      life

that almost was

but never

really.

Down,

    Lord

    if you get

    into this poem

    the editor

will be offended.

Under any circumstances

babies

(being people)

    are supposed to live

    not die.

    I feel so soft

    like crying

yet again (how do I

tell you, my two

dear friends)

thin

    and silver

    as moonlight

    dancing

    among clouds.

                     (Stillbirth; 2 May 1973)

MATTHEW'S MOON

Where
Does value lurk
in the ridiculous dying
of a child?
Not a child, no,
a baby not one day old.

The moon in the afternoon
and it isn't June.
Just like the moon in the afternoon
it shouldn't be,
no.

There lives no value in death
one only, one death only
had value
one lonely death and that
was only a kind of dying,
not like this but
Once there occurred a birth
which was a miracle

big like

a star outglowing the sun

making pale moths to sing for joy

and waking up children to dance.

Then, this time, there was the moon

glimpsed in the blue smoky

sky of afternoon

soon to be swallowed by night,

briefly triumphant

with lasting joy

To break the shackles of gloomy

everyday expectation

canonized in all the poets

by every oldwife in any town.

They almost got you down

but his birth is with you forever.

ONE FLESH

In the Beginning

My body was made

For your body.

We found when we met

That we fitted

Together

So finely we

Have never come

Unstuck.

Why should we?

You are the exact

Dimensions of

The hollow

In

My heart

VERY FUNNY POEM HA HA

**(Dedicated to contemporary images
of how it is)**

Gnashing teeth

vaginal

she slavering stands

yielding, he thrusts

into her breeches

an enchanted want.

Their enemy flesh

bangs

     in the dark

As they clash. They do not

come together

but

they do come

apart

(forever

              (Jan '74)

BINARY

Wind of your breathing,
starlight
    right before
and after
    your love.
    lightly dance
like a water strider
on ponds of starlight & mist.

Prowled hungry like a sleek
green-furred jaguar
    seeking
reality
    where fronds
    beat the moon gong.
Moon answered;
Your voice.

10,000 GREEN GALAXIES ON THE ONE SIDE OR EATING A PEANUT BUTTER SANDWICH ON THE OTHER

In my present madness

(thank you

     For this birthday

        present

   every day)

I see

flowers growing

    behind your eyes.

   nobody loves

tomorrow

so

I will celebrate

    living

      always

   and never never

certainly never

when

   but

in my present madness

  (I say

your eyes delight me

and your insides are my

     meds).

BILLBOARD IN THE SKY

(All God's conmen got connections
        what know bigtime angels who
   lay the truth on them
alone
        for a
                price)

only   tycoon saints can wash white
        your   deepseated elephants
                time   barnacles
and other
                vermin
that infest the modern-day god.

NY GUNMETAL JUNE

          I.   II.   III.

     Uptight   Incinerator Summer

city. The   seed fluff   bummer

     rigid   drifting   humid

galaxies shrink   everywhere

                              bean soup's

     from   without   sneak

     their neighbor in   a smile.
                              Preview in the

     professional   Wind-up   gently

     death.   dolls doing

                              choking smog.

     battle for the sidewalks

                                        pick

     gloom sprouts.

IN THE REALWORLD 11/20/82

In the RealWorld they're very

religious as you can see,

it's clear at least it's clear to me

out here

they really do worship the almighty dollar

in the RealWorld they strut in glory

high ruby cheeks,

high priced clothes and faces;

not "women" but "girls"

precious jewels

in leather and velvet.

In the RealWorld they move so slick and steady

Mercedes gliding by,

no eye contact.

Expressions all

exactly like yours

would be if you had a sea urchin up your ass.

In the RealWorld you just can't win

you can only run

after whoever is running

in front of you, while taking care

to keep ahead of those who run behind

COMMERCIAL MYRTLE MEETS BOUNCING BAZOOKAMAN

Skip-hop

        skip-hop

    skip-hop/

We( )re here

        because we( )re here

    because (skip

hip

hip

hooray/hiccup, little people, it's disaster

        time again

      with Uncle Human

    and his charming Foibles)

From the makers of

    bowelmovemend

      comes New Improved

      Orange-scented Ishkabibble (skip)

      Isn't it

        delicious?

FLICK

FLICK

      FLICKFLICKFLICKLET

      MEOUTLETME

      OUTOUT HELPMEHELPME

      PLEASEIWANNAGO

      HOME

_____

               (And here it is/

      Vajra-Prana

          with his zap-zap-zooper

hit

I Doan Need God an I Doan Need the Devil Neither Cuz

      I Kin Be Ugly

    All by Myself) hop(

) hop(

) hop

OR, YOU'D NEVER BELIEVE

    WHO I MET

        ON THE WAY TO THE TANTRA

FUNDAMENTAL EXERCISES IN THE CATAPULTIAN LOGIC

The marks
miss the mark

The marks, missing the mark,
hit the Marxist.

Even the Marxist
misses the mark;

Marks miss marks
Marxists miss Marx

Therefore
Marx is a mark or

All Marxists are marks,
too.

(Welcome, dear mark,
 To the chicken coop)

I WON'T BUY MY LIGHTNING FROM JUST ANY GROCERY

Take

the wind wild

stuff it not into a baggie!

What? She jerked upright

caught in the act.

GENESIS (AS CORRECTED BY THE POET)

There's a scarcity of
Golden creatures

And a surplus
of mud

Let me build an Average
Citizen

GOLDEN FLOWER

Golden Flower is dead

she died

               in the whirlwinds

when our universe came undone

But not of drugs.

This is the first time I have ever seen a dream's corpse

There were maggots in the lotus I recall

Metamorphosis

into the dreams of now –

The cancer has metastasized our patient is riddled

with hate

        amphetamine, heroin, bad acid and death.

The Coroner's verdict was

passion

           overdose of youth and hope

and

        Foolishness perhaps but Golden

Flower is dead.

SKY WRITHING

Sky

      sky

            fingers in the sun hair

golden body in

         the sky

             sky

fondling her clouds

Why

      why

            laughter on the breeze lips

passion in the wind arms of

         the sky

            why

he's kissing her

My

      o my

            sucking on the nipples of rain

Squirting in the warm flesh of

         the sky

            o my

they aren't married!

ANIMAL CRACKERS

The sun

is

a burning animal

    The moon

    a

    refrigerated star. Your

Love's

fresh strawberry

ice cream

    And I

    am

    a hot little child.

NEW MILLENNIUM

ON LOOKING BACK AT MY FIRST MARRIAGE

We are both very stubborn, yes
and I clearly have a
tendency to avoid confrontation,

even with myself (negative feelings?
swallow them)
taking chances, taking risks

(not physical so much
as of the existential kind),
close my eyes, grit my teeth,

let go inside, put it in parentheses
and breathe, do self-hypnosis,
numbly just apply a bit more effort,

plunge on ahead with the task in hand,
making life a hamster wheel.
You've had visions of a future,

You wanted to travel

retire by 50

have fun, see the world

Me, I was mired in the now.

I've accomplished lots but paid

for it in tunnel vision

(and the equivalent in feelings –

tunnel feelings?).

Just keep on truckin' as our friend Robert the

Cartoonist sez, and before I know it,

years (no, decades, three

decades) have passed.

I finally opened up,

collided

with all those consciously forgotten

Placed-in-parentheses feelings, bypassed

issues, unspoken shit.

And here we are

Parsecs apart, black matter dividing

galaxies drifting

alone in and by ourselves

SYZYGY

I.   Lover (now deceased)

You're a cuddler,

She said

Disappointedly

Pouted

Turned aside

And slept

Yes

I've always lusted for bodily fulfillment,

Touch

Motion

Sex and

Release but

Most deeply for

What comes next

(Or might

Or could,

Said my heart,

Come next)

II.   Spouse (now remarried)

Your pleasure is my joy

But still I yearn

Don't say us, or we

She said

Emphatically

It's you and it's me and we're separate people

Put her eye mask on

Turned aside

And slept

YesI've always lusted

For mutuality

Dreamt of sharing

Mind

And soul

And skin and flesh but

Mainly

Most deeply for

What comes next

(Or might

Or could

Whispered my heart)

A still soft voice

Come next...

Your joy is my pleasure

But mind's the gap

Intergalactic space

Cold, dark

Energy, a business proposition

III Miracle (sudden incursion of hands)

And then

Halfway through my fifth decade

All unexpected

You

I'd long given up

Except

in dreams

and yearning

You

our fingers knew first

You

our flesh got the notion

Hearts touched

You

The void

flipped into fullness

A boundless moment

a bounty of moments

of We

of Us and

I don't know where

You end and I begin

We slept

Sharing a dream

Us, we, you, me

Honestly,

I couldn't care less

Your joy is my pleasure

Your pleasure is my joy

ARTSGATO

How do I sing

Of love

and not come off all saccharine

and icky?

How do I write

happy poems

and not lose my audience

entirely?

Screw it. I'm happy.

I'm in love. I found everything I ever

wanted in the way

you hold a glass of wine,

your freckled cheek,

impertinent, knowing smile, the small of your back and

that nameless space behind your knee

VOWS

Kathryn

I shall be yours in all ways, always, so long as I have breath

Kathryn,

I give you my life, my love, my faithfulness and my trust

Kathryn,

keep my soul well, for I give it into your most gentle and loving care

Kathryn,

it took a lifetime to find you, and I swear to never abandon nor neglect you,

Kathryn,

always to be mindful, with open heart and eyes and hands

Kathryn,

never seek to control you, never to harm, never anything but my utmost, my very best

Kathryn,

I am yours, for whatever it is worth, wherever time and destiny, chance or fortune lead, I will be true

Kathryn,

let us be wed, let us walk together in the light, let us become the light, comets in love, trailed by joy

Kathryn,

let us dance together through the night, through rain and sun and snow and soar

Kathryn,

together on the currents of time and wonder, across the unfolding paths of tomorrow

Kathryn,

let us go now, laughing uproariously, together into the next chapters and volumes of our lives

Kathryn,

with tenderness and delight, whatever may come, I am yours; let you be mine and my joy is complete

REALIZATION OF A DREAM (FOR KATHRYN)

I thought I was not unhappy

at least content

or maybe numb because for all my life before (not since, not since)

there was a hole in my heart

Shaped precisely like your soul

how odd, I dreamed of she whom I now recognize as you

decades ago, a red-headed artist who would love me

and make me whole, as you do, as you do

Beloved, although my dream was

shorter than reality has proven to be,

not nearly so vivid

not nearly as strong, nor as in all ways lovely,

And so, despite the universe between, despite

time and distance and improbability we met

I could not keep my hands from seeking yours out to hold,

nor my heart to quest, to quest

For your gentleness forever

and your love and trust

and strength, your beauty and joy that follows wherever
you

Go. I no longer wait for it all to be over, but rather for
what further miracle should happen next

(Our wedding
Little Cayman
2 November 2005;
In a circle of conch shells
And candles))

I NEVER HAD A MONSTER

I never had a monster
under my bed
but I did have
three recurrent nightmares:

Turtles
sliding into a rocky creek all crowded with huge
unfriendly, technicolor
sliders, side necks, spiny nose, snappers

Wolf dog in my three years old closet
shaggy, dark brown, enormously
tall, slavering, soundless
crazy animated eyes

Flub-A-Dub from Howdy Doody (illuminated from within)
pops out from the wall laughing hysterically
goldfish dancing tailwise round the cuckoo clock
singing hickory dickory dock

OH FICKLE FINGER

It all comes round again

less a matter of

karma

or Ecclesiastes, purpose,

yuga, kalpa or whatever

turning of Aeon's wheel

than

spitefully to haunt you.

So get your finger out of my face

and leave me be

CREATION MYTH (OR IS IT MYTHUS?)

Goddess

Sat on her pot

and shat

the universe.

Stop

taking things

so seriously,

dammit.

TESSELLATION

Patterns patterns

         everywhere

   and not

             a thought

to think

PILED HIGHER AND DEEPER, YES INDEED

I am

a sociologist

which means (read my textbook)

I'm an expert

on everyone else's business, and (check the citations)

master

of jack shit

METAMORPHISM

I have become
a consumer

Of other people's imaginations
a form

Of death
one of those little deaths or,

Rather,
            fossilization

Of the mens poesis
egg

Caterpillar
butterfly

Me
oh.

My mind was wandering off on a drowse

an inch of the way

through The Dragon's Flight

Volume 12 of The Battle for Light

Damn.

shaking the spiderwebs out of my head,

I put my book down,

having marked the page with

A business card

and boot up my computer

NARRATIVE COSMOLOGY

It all fits together

into a story

but always in present time

first person

unfolding

INNOCENT OF EXPERIENCE

Blake hated

science for its

mechanistic rapine of reality

but he

made etchings

which, of course,

is a very technical process

WILLIAM BLAKE'S iMAC

Poets long

have rued

the onslaught of science

left-brained rationality

commerce consumerism

cold hard cash

bankers, o god, bankers

bean counters

hedge fund neuro-

marketers

the measurement of dreams

parsing of the heart

grey little men

bigger pinker C-level

dickheads

in their perfectly tailored

C-level suites

but

they, too,

are made of atoms, quarks and strings and other

stuff whose very existence

is rooted in the fine brown earth

of mystery

just like rough and

smooth-barked trees

stellar jays all glistening black/blue

fallen needles,

still-green leaves,

and fat-tailed salamanders

hiding under old rail trestles in my yard

fishes and frogs

turtles (snapping and box)

bears, wolves, beans,

and small annoying bitey things all

with their place in the ecosystem

along with those fucking right-wngers

Me,

while I like acoustic instruments

I love electric music, too.

PAINFUL VOID

Painful void

trembles in

anticipation of

approach, shuddering

at the risks

and ecstasies,

the prospect

of becoming

a plenum

REALITY HURTS

I'd like to be profound
but I'm not
I'm really quite simple

I'd like to be a true gourmand
but I'm not
I just like stuff that tastes good

I'd like to be a connoisseur of wine
but I'm not
My palate just knows what it likes, however déclassé

I'd like to be the hero of your story
I'd like to be on the cover of Time Magazine
I'd like to be the One who saves the universe

vanquishes evil, establishes (or helps
establish) a truly fair and just
and life-affirming social order that

pays the universe back for my existence

and the air I breathe

but I'm not

I'm just…

I don't know what –

      I've got a great rearview mirror

and long-distance wisdom

a shitload of half-formed dreams

and implicit expectations

Oh well…

Time to put my tongue back firmly

in cheek, and seem so cool, and be –

Oh shit… I just bit down on it

OUCH!

Reality hurts.

ONCE I WAS A POET

Once, I was a poet
(fancied) young
belly full of cummings, Yeats and Blake and
Pound
Aiken, Ginsberg, Ed Sanders and myself,
     my greenhorn self;   my oh my
          my pale green horny jeanclad
        engineer-booted moustache-growing
        high minded
    space-facing
college student postadolescent visionary
self (and savior of the human race
of course)
then
I knew the secret: it was not the first word
     nor the second word but
the poem
That is the image of god in man
Today, I am a scientist
(social) not so young

skull crammed with Weber, Marx and Mead and Mills, Durkheim, Parsons,

Blumer

Goffman, W.I. Thomas and myself,

    if anything too much myself,

        neither reconciled nor awakened,

           verdigris and Peter Pan

           bluebottles

    buzzing on flypaper hanging from the ceiling

(nobody's savior, not even my own) rapidly

depleting my stash of tomorrow, and too damned little

now

I know the truth (and it's a question):

    it was not the first word

        nor the second word but

the song

What is the image of god in man?

AFTER SOLSTICE THE NEW YEARS' LOOM

Less always than never

more sometimes than might

we stretch from earliest twinklings

of certain because, striding

surely, eternals laughing

through yet tomorrows' wakening

oh the dreams, the dreams, the dream so

free of been and known and the shit

that happened to happen despite

or perhaps because

we grasped perfection's image,

blinding ourselves with light.

how we all so bright and certain

so small and huge and high, stupid, petty

and gloriously untainted as the sun reflected

in Lucy's diamond sky on the soles

of our shoes, bare feet,

Beatles boots and sandals

no fog back then, even in San Francisco

no clouds, no buts, no stultifying clauses,

red purple sky and the magic show

of headlights streaming on the building side

across the empty lot beside where I lived,

next door to the Family Dog, occasionally

Scoring lids from Martune the Magician.

Mystery was there, aplenty, undarkened

shiny empty rooms awaiting occupancy

forever dew sparkling out before us

like a magic carpet ride or riders we

had, of course, our certainty

our postures, cynical stances, our coolth,

far outs, no ways, why nots

our booze, our music and our drugs

poems and meditations, marches,

sit ins, stand ins, pomposity and skinny

naked smiles, our auditing, our asanas, our oms

and now what have we left but

one another, sharp swift glimpsing hints

of evers yet remaining,

a creak here, ache there, giggle and groan

haunted memories of future dreams

we shall not fail, we bright beings that we

still be, tarnished somewhat by rude time and

facticity, experience, breakable, unbroken,

we persist, and cannot help but and do

for after Solstice, the new years loom

joy, again, winking glimpses through the cracks

of onrushing, tangent evers,

the dooms and hopes of futures past

stalking tangos of not yet but shall

or maybe a rhumba of perhaps (Death, go

fuck yourself, wait over there, in a corner,

please)

NOT AN APOLOGIA

I tried

many things

stuck with some

SCUBA, ballroom, rock and roll

5-strong banjo and marriage

cannabis, more than 50 years

Fantasy and science fiction: Cordwainer

Smith, Dr. Who and Terry Pratchett

Music, mainly Americana, some UK

Rutles and Bonzo, the Rolling Stones,

Renbourne's guitar and Richard Thompson's,

Maddy Prior, June Tabor, Jaqui McShee...

Most anything twice, more if I like it

others but once

like heroin

(Itched me to death, mellow yes, but

spiraling down the cosmic drain proved

not my bliss)

I tried to believe

many things

"faith in things unseen" didn't work for me

Nor did shut up and go with the flow, but

some things I do believe

"there's a light that is shining in the heart of the world"

As Sydney Carter and Pastor Chuck

had it

yes

And song

and poetry

irony and satire and

Most

of all

love

TOO MUCH OF A GOOD THING

Leaves in forest

stretching out

thrusting greenly to the sun

enthralled

glorious in spring

shrivel in the summer heat and sun

P.O.V.

Some people take the world literally

not me

figurative all the way

down

ask my turtle

8-19-17 DEPARTURE TO PLACES UNKNOWN

8-19

her birthday

8:19

her last breath...

Only Pattie could do that

in her perpetual certainty and

joy

even toward the very last, a joke

Sucking on a popsicle

orange, I think it was....

long trembling fingers raised

it to her mouth

With difficulty, yes, but still

that never-leaving smile

she loved wine and

she loved the blues,

Loved her daughters, grandchild Bella,

long

term friends (from kindergarten even),

an ecology of laughter

even when her body turned against her

the laughter remained front and center

her Prada bags

despite

Her spirit standing tall, unwavering

independence

pure, unadulterated

100%

herself...

Too many friends have left the road

taken the Ausfahrt

to places unknown...

ave atque vale (mixed metaphors and all)

ENOUGH ALREADY

Enough already

With time

And Trump

And technology; how

About life

And love

And laughter?

Pluck a string

Let the jello tremble

Time to be human or just plain be:

Not male

Nor female

Not old, not young/

Born again

Or again and again

Millennial

Boomer

Cis or trans or ... who the fuck cares?

Let's stage a jailbreak

Leap the fence!

Tunnel out from all those categories!

Snuggle into quantum uncertainty!

Mmmm good...

Back to the uncarved block

Gate gate Bodhi

Svaha

And hoohah!

Caterpillar, butterfly, light

At the center of the void

Gravity waves tickle

Dark matter

The dance begins

Joi de vivre

Jollity and

Joy

(Enough already)

SIR DOUGLAS

Semi-Rampant,

Slate gray/brown above

Fox red below

Sir Douglas,

Squirrel

Madly darts

Down vine to feeder full

Of black oil sunflower,

Beige peanuts, yellow corn

Twitching

Amidst a flurry of nuthatches

Gorgeous little black and white birds

Some with orange bellies

Just like Sir Douglas...now,

Quick,

Down

From feeder to

Pre-dug

Flower pot hole

Deposits exactly 3 kernels of corn

Back to trellis

Up, top of fence

Mouth munching

Stand guard, rampant again

Tail bushed out, look fierce

(Or fierce as you can, at 10 inches on a good day)

Chitter, chirp

Back to feeder, chase away

Big blueblack stellar jay

Dart

Down and back to cache more corn

In another hole.

Close it over

Forget it, back to fence.

Ignore that silly brown wrentit,

Ground birds, hah!

Twitch

Grab some peanuts,

Snag some corn,

Lord of the yard

And don't you forget it, buster,

C'mere, I'll stare you down I'll fluff my tail

I'll... oh hell, you've come too close

Run away and yell

At you from down the fence ...

Oh, by the way,

Can I have some more seeds

In the feeder, please?

APPROACHING 4/20

I feel like flotsam

On the banks of time

When I was a teenager I didn't drive a fancy car to school

I hopped the fence

And walked up the hill, all the way,

Even in Winter

(Ok, a quarter mile; it's the principal that counts)

If they'd let me use a calculator (if there even were calculators)

I'd be a hard scientist today

If I had a smartphone then or YouTube

I coulda gone viral,

Made a mint, maybe even wore a suit and tie and felt that was me

Gotten onto the cover of Time Magazine

Und so Weider

Et cetera

Tao ke tao fei chang tao (if

I remember correctly)

Our cherry tree is covered in a magnificence

Of white blossoms with

Just a hint of pink

It's gnarled, it's old, it doesn't care, has no regrets

JUST LIKE THAT

How easily

We slide

From simile

To metaphor

As if

The world were

My oyster

And I was

A pearl

MARGINALIST MANIFESTO, AGNOSTIC PRAYER OR SIMULATION THEREOF

Lived near the Haight – student, no hippie, self-impressed

Longish hair, paisley shirt, electric blue widewale cords
engineer boots, black –

Assumed we were (collectively) over it, the revolution
had come, was coming all around Us (wipe that

Picture out of your mind,

R.Crumb orgiast I wish, but wasn't)

Watching and yearning, not quite partaking

I read poetry at the Artist Liberation Front's Free Fair in the
Panhandle...

Typewriter slinger, no guitar,

Truth was, I couldn't hack it, too intense

Boundaries aquiver, a risk too far

Scared me shitless in fact, so I held back

A bullshit bodhisattva

(And, in any case, no club asked me to join)

Pass that reefer round

So I got jaded (what with the speed and all the partying

Acid-heads

Disciples of a new Dionysus, parishioners of the

Marketeering priests of Hip)

Tried to get out of this place.

Spring free (om followed by several

Years of embarrassment too pathetic to relate)

On reflection, I think I'd just discovered

(As I fear all too many have done)

The secret of pretention...

OK. Found some joy and some fulfillment

Left some minor legacy among too damn

Many ever-quickening

Circumnavigations of the sun

Now, time-dizzied, dehypnotized, ridden by loas

Shame and Regret,

Scales fallen from my eyes only to see we'd

Trashed the downpressing structures of old and

Left...

What?`

Faith still abided we'd all turned a corner

Forward, backward, sideways, down, slip and

Slide but incrementally

Always trending up and out,

Llike flowers tracking the burnt umber sun on a fog-filled day

And then came Trump

And Ryan, Pence, McConnell and all their smiling bland-faced, bilious bunch,

Populism for the masses while stepping on

Their faces (it's a leg up)

Hands folded in prayer.

Midwives of a new era, folks, Age of the

Financiers and Owners of Software

Praise be to their multithousanddollar suits,

Cool Silicon Valley

Undress-to-impress

Bentleys and top-tier Teslas we can't possibly afford,

But wouldn't it be nice?

Their lovely wives au couture, and, most of all, their bank accounts offshore

Red-capped worshippers thrusting their fists, prostrating their spirits,

Squawking like starlings

Sacrificing their selves at the altar of

The 1%

(Digitized, of course – very slickly done I must confess)

Psalms of the mass market, false consciousness uber Alles!

Back to the blues, I guess.

Protest songs, your time has come again.

Take up your instruments,

Raise your voices

On with the pussy hats

And sing.

Practice satire as long as we're still allowed

And here to hassle (touch of gray fading white)

The powerful, smug, self-righteous.

Never doubt (or, at least, so try)

The tide will turn, the light return,

As we come to the longest days of the year,

Let us pray to Whomever or Whatever

Wherever, I or thou or all together:

May we live to see another human spring

(And maybe break this infernal, eternal cycle

Hope to

Despair, beauty

To mass market replicates of someone else's joy)

Here, on Earth,

Where

We're stuck for the duration.

4-22, VICTORIA B.C.

Silver and blue

Balloon said 70

Table besides ours

Full of family cheer

I went over and said to the man

In the paper crown all glittery

Silver and blue,

Hello

Is today your birthday?

He said yes,

And I said

Young man,

Congratulations

(I'm 2 days Older) and

He grinned and he said

          We're too old

To die young

JustSpring's gone

And summer

Fall will come

But for now, let's go back

To our hotel room

Snuggle, smoke

And (yes, we still can do it you

Wonderful gorgeous

Woman my wife)

Let's screw.

LAST I HEARD SHE WAS HANGING WITH PIGPEN

Are you still alive out there

Somewhere

Now in your 60s?

No longer jailbait

As when I met you,

Rescued you from the ambulance coming

To take you away

You couldn't work, legs all swollen up from those net
stockings but

You needed to work and were required to wear them

But you couldn't so

You lay on your bed trembling

Had been there for days

The starving, strungout couple whose place you crashed
at had

Lost all patience and placed that call...

So I took you in

Your Hollywood face

Your full and gorgeous breasts you said

You used to hang out with Ginsberg and Ferlinghetti
(they

Named you Princess, you said; we thought you lied)

Princess, you came on to Tom and me

"Two such lovely men" you said grinning with come-on eyes

And freaked us out.

Somehow eased you out, don't remember how and

When you returned around Christmas you

Said you'd done a movie with Peter, Paul

And Mary in which you had sex

With Super Spade (before the Hells Angels got him) – we thought you lied

"Jailbait, mad, stay away" and, besides, I was leaving soon and,

Let's face it, too uptight....

Years later I saw an old Playboy and it had

A review of a movie, not too good,

By Peter, Paul and Mary in which

It said "a voluptuous blonde

Screwed Super Spade

On the beach"

Once I had a miracle in my arms and in my bed and

Disbelieved and lost.... Who knows?

Was everything true?

Another fork in the road not taken

Where might it have led?

PDX TO ATLANTA VIA PHX

Lonesome Sunday flying off

For work. All these years

Over 2 million miles

In the air and until now

I have never written a poem on

An airplane,

Winging for work.

Should have taken the opportunity in the good old days

When flying was fun and I was frequent

And my homelife was stale so I lived

In the air, up front,

Where I could at least open a laptop fully not hunched
over my screen

At some weird angle

This pitch in coach squeezed in , body

And mind somehow hurtling across the continent in a
metal

Cigar tube with wings

Worst airplane meal I've had in maybe 30 years

Cold BBQ chicken on a ciabatta desert

Fittingly made in Phoenix,

Dry, inedible

... A fitting metaphor

For the America unfolding below

(Every row

Has closed their window so we cannot see

The truth of this burning summer's land

Days of climate change and vodka

Large vacationers in flipflops, Bluetooth earbuds and shorts

Watching movies on tiny screens – isolated, alone

Virtual life, not actual)

I don't like being so far from my darling. Let me imagine

Banjos in the hollers, guitars in the cottonfields above which we pass

People together playing lovesongs, ballads and the blues

PHILLY METRO SUMMER MEMORY

O boy,

That time again…

On with the leash

Open the door

Sunglasses steam up

Instantaneously,

Her first hot

Muggy

Mid-Atlantic

Cicada-screaming

Summer's day

Sydney (long haired

Blue merle border collie

AKA "Beautiful"

Veteran of Nevada's dry

Comstock heat

That can fry an egg on the sidewalk)

Sticks her nose out the door...

Brown eye

Blue eye

Dilate in panic

Turns to us,

Nose wrinkled, eyes wide

"What the fuck?"

CRAZYTOWN

Crazytown!

Orange demigod grabbing

Headlines and pussy

Tweeting bullshit, invective and lies

Heartless capitalism

Red hats and crosses, eyes modestly downcast

And not just to avoid the dirty needles

Miscellaneous shit

Castoff humans

Tents along the highway

Rusted mountain bikes

Shopping carts piled

With the grubby stuff of homeless lives

"It's a moral requirement to make money

When you can...

To sell product for the highest price"

Ferragamo wingtips, Louboutin sneaks

Healthcare bankruptcies

A bubble tea age

Fast food, microwave pizza, glamping and

Three hundred dollar tasting menus (wine pairing extra)

Bacon habanero ice cream, Millennial angst

(There's an app for it)

Keep your stockholders happy, pump that value, short that stock,

Holding signs on the onramps, God Bless

Fraying flip flops, Jimmy Choos

Black Suede Pointy Toe Pumps with Crystals and Feathers

Free shipping if you click here to purchase online

Put it on your credit card (What's in YOUR wallet?

1% cash back on everything all the time

Buy a new smartphone

Every day (Got a really cool OLED screen 10 zillion colors, same price as those shoes)

At least you can buy your weed at a retail dispensary

Most anywhere in Oregon

And they wonder why Boomers

Are lining up at the counters

Edibles, oils, plastic canisters and cash in hand (hint:

It's not the 10% discount for old farts like me)

I've lived in New York, I've lived in San Francisco but now

We're all here doing what we can to

Do what we should,

Biding our time

Dreaming of deorangification

In Crazytown

TINY HANDS (THREE YEARS IN)

Hardworking people

Salt of the earth

Conned once again

By the perfectly stable

Functionally illiterate

Cheeseburder scarfing

Evangelist-anointed

Bigly, sadly, unimpeachable (it's

A dirty word) fast tweetin'

Ex-New-York-City, now-Floridian

Orange-faced, covefe tootin'

Flim-flam man.

DONE, JUST DONE

No plans

To reincarnate

(Hope-

Fully I'm done

With all that shit)

TOMORROW I WILL BE PRIME AGAIN

Last day of my 70th year

Feeling meditative,

    Introspective

        (Understandably)

Always marginal

    Seeking

        Hoping

            Dreaming

                Of breakthrough

Into the comfort of belonging, not standing

Alone

    In the cold fluorescent light

            Of mechanical unlife.

Had two great loves

    The first probably more

    One-sided,

        Driven by

    My impulse to belong

We danced to the Doors in the Antioch Union

    Our first evening together

    Me just 18

"Break on through to the other side"

And I kept trying

Driven by ego

And impetuousness, a bit of snobbery, Fear

Of ridicule and imperfection

I think I was unteachable

And very slow on the human uptake

But good at taking a deep breath

And hanging in, keeping on

Keeping on

Always at the margins

Groucho Marxian

A shitty student with A+ Grades

But good learner albeit somewhere mildly "on

The spectrum"

Good with words,

Better than with people.

Maybe thanks to a mother who never got the

Meaning of that word

Soft and cuddly, no

Trapped in her own,

Holocaust-ridden early teens

Dachau got her parents,

Though she got away more less

Unscathed

Except in psyche

And a dad

Self-educated genius

But German, very German

The German kind of German Jew

Hard working, built a small

Fortune by sheer pluck

And smarts.... A true Mensch but

His world was concentric circles,

Pretty closed, family is all

Outgroups just don't count

Keep your head down,

Maintain control

His life was his Business

His business was

His life

Never take a vacation unless you can

Combine it with

Work

Out the door in the morning

Back in the Evening, Then repeat

Turned me against being a

Salesman I tell you or a businessman

Of any sort.

But anyhow

My mother wanted me to be an

"Intellectual"

Among the "Literati"

The future she'd imagined for

Herself that

Was stolen by Hitler

(I suspect this was a

Source of contention; he just

Wanted a "real Straus")

Short story entitled

"Childhood on a microscope Stage"

Don't bother to read it

Painful and boring

I neglected learning German, strived

To become a full-fledged American

First-generation in a second- and third-

Generation neighborhood,

Well

It sucked

My escape was the woods behind

Our house, the old Phipps Estate all overgrown,

Unkempt,

 Blooming buzzing green and brown

  And books,

  Books, books, books

  And Books

A theoretical youth

 55 years to find true

  True love

  That is,

   Kathryn who loves me for me

   Myself

Got here the long way round

 Break on through to the other side

  Slowly or at least try

 Student, counterculture, more

  Head than acid freak

   Psychedelics Saved my

 Soul, I

  Must confess, but I

Couldn't get beyond that membrane of me

 Just join in and squirm around in an

Egoless pile

Of bodies like puppies,

Just couldn't let go,

But I tried And I tried

And like

The Fugs' Reverend Kenny Weaver

Just couldn't get High,

At least not that way.

Got into yoga when it all turned to speed

Hari om nama!

Hari Om nama!

(The mantram Satchidananda

Gave to me)

Doing asanas

Five hours a day, shunning

Sweets and

Eating rice trying

So hard to get out

Before I learned to be here now

(Oh

The pompous stupidity of impatient youth)

Dianetics then Scientology when

I got bored

And wanted a short-cut

        But they didn't take to a Marginalist

           And I was incapable

       Of letting myself go, In any case

    Corrected with a spot of Jesus but that

Didn't work for me, either

      It's like trying to fall asleep

        Closer and closer Asymptotically

  But Never quite

Reaching the other side

  Still, I've never surrendered

    Stood back, a bit chickenshit, but

Doing my part as best

      I can toward healing

        The world

  Leaving it better than when

    I was dragged into It (by C-Section)

    Reimbursing the universe for the

Loan of experience

      Faint visions of fog-Shrouded
Mountains

      In deep time

    Whispers of the Mahayana

Realization, long ago, that my

Dharma is

Not grandiosity (I'll never be on the

Cover of Time Magazine) but

Learn to get it right

This time.

Attend to the here

And now.

That's my job,

Tikkun olam.

Change the world in little ways,

By acts of living softly

And with love.

I think I'm getting there

I hope I am

But feeling old today

Meditative

Introspective

The world seems to be turning its back

On our long-embraced

Once counterculture now "progressive"

Humanist dreams of arcing

Toward liberty, unity

And sharing the gifts

      Of life on this little mudball

Circling through space and time.

 Was it,

      Like those pinstripe elders scoffed in their

Hats and ties and

      Perforated wingtip brogues

      Just a youthful illusion?

      Doesn't matter

      Joy lies in breaking Through

From me and you

      To the other side,

            To us,

      Together,

      In the little acts

Of compassionate living

      In Gentleness.

PRIME AGAIN

My poems, my life so far were all written

Before the Plague,

The year our sky turned brushfire orange

And we were told

Be prepared to pack and flee,

Before the great February ice storm of '21

That stripped so many trees

Naked here in West Linn,

Before the heat dome that left us literally

Hotter than hell (or anywhere else on Earth),

Before January 6th and QAnon

And all those white people on McLoughlin

Under a redwhite&blue striped canopy just across

The Willamette River, maskless, flying flags, boiling

Eyes, anti-Vax, tears of rage and hurt and loss,

Crying for the impeachment of rationality, Justice

For Ashley Babbitt,

Stop Child Trafficking, Jesus, Jesus,

Jesus,

Calling for Trump's return;

73 and I want a re-do (like in a video game)

UNEXPECTED BENEDICTION

I spoke to her that afternoon...
Caregiver put the phone
To Mother's ear

"I called to say I love you"
(As I'd said almost daily all that year -
Didn't expect her to reply)

"I love you too" she responded,
Garbled, faint, an unexpected benediction,
But I heard

I heard and shortly after, I am told,
She closed her eyes,
Went to sleep

And stopped.
It was the Spring solstice
Longest day of the year (and shortest night

Made in the USA
Middletown, DE
21 September 2021